THE CENTENNIAL STATE BUCKET LIST
100 DESTINATIONS YOU MUST VISIT

COLORADO

TRAVEL GUIDE

DIANA L.
MITCHELL

Table of Contents

Dear reader, thanks a lot for purchasing by book.

As you're about to find out, this guide comes with several maps to guide you through the roads of beautiful Colorado.

However, to help you plan your trip even more efficiently, I have included an interactive map powered by Google My Maps.

To access it, scan the QR code below.

Happy travelling!

Introduction

Welcome to *Colorado Travel Guide*, your ultimate guide to exploring the vast landscapes and hidden gems of the Centennial State. From the historic charm of Durango, where the past meets the present, to the natural splendor of the Rocky Mountains, this guide uncovers the myriad attractions Colorado has to offer.

Our journey commences in the Front Range. Stroll through the historic streets of Fort Collins, or immerse yourself in the aromatic world of the Celestial Seasonings Tea Factory in Boulder. Each destination, from the awe-inspiring Red Rocks Park and Amphitheatre to the serene Cherry Creek State Park, offers a distinct experience of Colorado's dynamic character.

Venturing south, we uncover a collage of geological wonders and historical intrigue. Stand in awe at the towering formations of the Garden of the Gods in Colorado Springs, or delve into the military legacy of the United States Air Force Academy. The southern region harmonizes the rugged outdoors with rich historical narratives, presenting attractions like the Royal Gorge Bridge and Park and the captivating landscapes around Pikes Peak.

The heart of Colorado, the Denver Greater Area, pulses with a fusion of history, culture, and innovation. Explore the intellectual oasis of the Denver Museum of Nature & Science, enjoy a day out at the Denver Zoo, or catch a game at Coors Field. Denver's vibrant city life, set against the backdrop of the majestic Rockies, showcases the state's penchant for blending urban sophistication with natural splendor.

Our expedition leads us to the Rocky Mountains, where nature's majesty unfolds in places like Rocky Mountain National Park and the tranquil Bear Lake. This region, a paradise for outdoor enthusiasts, offers endless adventures from hiking and skiing to tranquil moments by alpine lakes.

Finally, the Western Slope reveals Colorado's rugged terrain and adventurous spirit. Discover the tranquil beauty of Hanging Lake, marvel at the geological formations in Colorado National Monument, or experience the tranquil waters of the Blue Mesa Reservoir. This area, with its diverse landscapes and outdoor activities, promises an unforgettable exploration of Colorado's wild side.

The *Colorado Travel Guide* is more than a collection of destinations; it's an invitation to experience the diverse beauty, history, and culture of Colorado. Each of these carefully selected destinations offers an authentic and memorable journey. So, pack your spirit of adventure and get ready to discover the wonders of Colorado like never before!

About Colorado

Landscape of Colorado

In *Colorado Travel Guide*, we explore not just the destinations but the stunning landscapes that frame them – the diverse and majestic terrains of Colorado. This chapter unveils the varied landscapes and natural marvels that make the Centennial State a treasure trove of the West's natural splendor.

Mountain Majesty: The Rockies and Beyond

Colorado is renowned for its section of the Rocky Mountains, offering a dramatic convergence of towering peaks, alpine lakes, and expansive forests. From the rugged, snow-capped summits of the Front Range to the serene beauty of the San Juan Mountains in the southwest, Colorado's mountainous terrain is a haven for outdoor enthusiasts and nature lovers. Iconic peaks like Pikes Peak and Mount Elbert serve as beacons for adventurers, while the state's numerous ski resorts transform these landscapes into winter wonderlands.

Urban Green Spaces and Rivers

Colorado's urban landscapes, particularly in Denver and Boulder, beautifully integrate green spaces and outdoor recreation. The Denver Botanic Gardens and Boulder's Chautauqua Park offer residents and visitors alike a touch of nature amidst city life. The South Platte River, winding through Denver, and Boulder Creek, flowing through Boulder, provide scenic settings for jogging, cycling, and waterside dining.

The High Plains and Eastern Colorado

The eastern part of the state showcases the vast, open landscapes of the High Plains. This region, with its rolling grasslands and wide horizons, offers a stark contrast to the mountainous west. The plains are rich in agricultural history and are dotted with small towns and communities that embody the spirit of the American frontier.

The Western Slope: Plateaus and Mesas

The Western Slope of Colorado, defined by the Colorado River and its tributaries, is characterized by its rugged plateaus, deep canyons, and mesas. This area includes the stunning landscapes of the Colorado National Monument and the vast, untamed beauty of the Mesa Verde National Park, with its ancient Puebloan cliff dwellings.

The Foothills and Valleys

Nestled between the plains and the peaks are Colorado's foothills and valleys, offering lush landscapes and fertile grounds for vineyards and orchards. The Cache la Poudre River Canyon, near Fort Collins, and the Roaring Fork Valley, near Aspen, are examples of the breathtaking beauty and recreational opportunities these areas provide.

In Conclusion

Colorado's landscapes are as varied as they are magnificent. From the iconic Rockies to the serene plains, from bustling city parks to the rugged Western Slope, the state's natural beauty is a vital part of its charm and appeal. As travelers explore these landscapes, they're invited to discover not just the backdrop but the heart and soul of Colorado.

The Flora and Fauna of Colorado

In *Colorado Travel Guide*, we journey beyond the urban landscapes into the heart of nature's bounty that Colorado so generously offers. This chapter is devoted to the rich diversity of flora and fauna that grace the landscapes of the Centennial State, painting a vivid picture of the ecosystems that flourish under its skies.

Flora: A Rich Palette

Colorado's flora reflects its varied topography and climates, from the arid plains to the lofty peaks of the Rockies. Each zone nurtures a distinct set of plant species that contribute to the state's stunning natural beauty.

Mountain Flora: In the high elevations, alpine tundra and subalpine forests prevail. Here, hardy species like the Colorado blue columbine (the state flower), Engelmann spruce, and subalpine fir withstand the harsh conditions. Wildflower meadows burst into a kaleidoscope of colors in the summer, with lupines, Indian paintbrushes, and sunflowers.

Plains and Valleys: The eastern plains and river valleys are adorned with grasslands and shrubs, including sagebrush and rabbitbrush, supporting a vast ecosystem of wildlife. The cottonwood and willow-lined riversides offer lush contrast to the grassy expanses.

Unique Plant Life: Among its ecological treasures, Colorado protects several endemic species, such as the Rocky Mountain bristlecone pine, known for its incredible longevity and resilience.

Fauna: A Symphony of Life

The animal kingdom in Colorado is as diverse as its landscapes, from the elusive lynx prowling the snowy mountain ranges to the bighorn sheep scaling steep cliffs.

Marine and Aquatic Life: While Colorado is landlocked, its rivers and lakes teem with life, including the rainbow trout and the greenback cutthroat trout, the state fish, thriving in its fresh waters.

Birds of Colorado: The state is a birdwatcher's paradise, hosting migratory species and residents alike. The bald eagle, peregrine falcon, and the Colorado state bird, the lark bunting, grace the skies and landscapes with their presence.

Mammalian Residents: Colorado's forests, plains, and mountains are home to a range of mammals from the majestic elk and moose to the secretive bobcat and mountain lion.

Preservation and Conservation

Colorado's dedication to preserving its natural heritage is evident in its numerous national parks, wildlife refuges, and conservation programs. Initiatives like the Colorado Natural Areas Program ensure the protection of both well-known and obscure species, maintaining the state's biodiversity for future generations.

In Conclusion

The flora and fauna of Colorado are integral to its identity, offering endless exploration and discovery opportunities. They not only embellish the state's landscapes but also play crucial roles in its ecological systems. As visitors traverse through Colorado's vast wilderness, they're invited to marvel at the living mosaic that thrives in this majestic state, reminding us of nature's resilience and beauty.

The Climate of Colorado

In *Colorado Travel Guide*, the climate is a key character in the story of each destination. This chapter explores the climate of Colorado, revealing its impact on the state's landscapes, biodiversity, and the quintessential Colorado travel experience.

Seasonal Variations: A Year-Round Adventure

Colorado's climate is as varied as its geography, ranging from semi-arid conditions to alpine climates at higher elevations, each bringing distinct seasons and unique experiences.

Spring (March to May): Spring in Colorado is a season of renewal, with warming temperatures melting the winter snows. The weather can be unpredictable, ranging from sunny days to late snow showers, especially in the mountains. This season invites the first hikes of the year, wildflower blooms at lower elevations, and the tail end of the ski season.

Summer (June to August): Summers are generally warm and sunny, with clear blue skies and occasional afternoon thunderstorms, particularly in the mountains. The higher altitudes offer a pleasant escape from the heat, making it a perfect time for hiking, camping, and exploring Colorado's natural parks and outdoor spaces.

Fall (September to November): Autumn is a spectacular season in Colorado, celebrated for its brilliant aspen golds and crisp air. It's an ideal time for scenic drives, mountain biking, and witnessing the state's famed fall foliage. The weather is cooler, especially in the evenings, as the state prepares for winter.

Winter (December to February): Colorado's winters are cold and snowy, particularly in the mountain regions, making it a world-renowned destination for skiing, snowboarding, and other winter sports. The snow-capped landscapes are stunning, offering a magical backdrop for winter adventures.

Regional Climate Differences

Mountain Areas: Higher elevations experience cooler temperatures year-round and significant snowfall in winter, perfect for Colorado's famous ski resorts.

Plains and Valleys: These regions see warmer summers and milder winters compared to the mountains, with varied precipitation.

Impact of Climate Change

Climate change is altering Colorado's landscapes, with noticeable effects on snowpack levels, wildfire frequency, and shifting seasonal patterns. These changes are closely monitored to mitigate impacts on Colorado's natural beauty and outdoor recreation industry.

Preparing for Travel

When planning a trip to Colorado, consider the diverse climate:

Spring and Summer: Prepare for warm days and cooler nights, with layered clothing and rain gear for sudden showers.

Fall: Bring layers to accommodate cool mornings and warmer afternoons, especially in the mountains.

Winter: Essential warm clothing, including insulated coats, hats, gloves, and waterproof boots, is necessary for snow activities.

In Conclusion

Colorado's climate enhances its allure, offering dynamic and diverse backdrops that shift with the seasons. Whether you're exploring the summer trails, marveling at autumn's colors, hitting the ski slopes in winter, or witnessing spring's renewal, understanding Colorado's climate enriches your visit, promising an unforgettable journey through the Centennial State's natural wonders.

The History of Massachusetts

In *Colorado Travel Guide*, history is not merely a backdrop but a core element that defines the state's essence. This chapter invites you on a voyage through time to uncover the rich historical fabric that has woven Colorado into the dynamic state it is today.

Indigenous Heritage and European Exploration

Long before European explorers set foot in the region, Colorado was home to numerous Native American tribes, including the Ute, Arapaho, and Cheyenne. Their deep connection with the land and rich cultural heritage significantly shaped Colorado's history.

The mid-19th century marked a new chapter with the arrival of European settlers and the beginning of exploration and mining expeditions. The discovery of gold in 1858 led to the Colorado Gold Rush, bringing a flood of prospectors to the area, which played a crucial role in Colorado's early development and statehood in 1876.

Center Stage in the American West

Colorado's strategic location at the heart of the American West made it a key player in the westward expansion, witnessing pivotal moments from the building of the transcontinental railroad to conflicts and treaties with Native American tribes.

Industrialization and Environmental Conservation

The late 19th and early 20th centuries saw Colorado emerge as an industrial powerhouse, with mining and agriculture shaping its economy. This era also saw the birth of the conservation movement, with figures like John Muir advocating for the preservation of Colorado's natural beauty, leading to the establishment of national parks and protected areas.

20th Century and Modern Era

Throughout the 20th century, Colorado continued to be a site of significant social and technological evolution. It played a substantial role in the space race and became a hub for scientific research and innovation, with institutions such as the United States Air Force Academy and the National Renewable Energy Laboratory.

Colorado has also been progressive in social policies, being among the first states to legalize marijuana for recreational use, reflecting its ongoing tradition of pioneering social change.

Historical Landmarks and Legacy

Colorado is scattered with historical landmarks that tell the story of its past. From the ancient cliff dwellings of Mesa Verde National Park to the historic mining towns like Leadville and the vibrant cultural heritage of Denver, these sites offer a portal into the past, allowing visitors to immerse themselves in Colorado's rich history.

In Conclusion

Grasping the history of Colorado is essential to fully appreciate its present. From its indigenous roots through its central role in the expansion of the West, to its status as a beacon of innovation and social progress, Colorado's history is a narrative of resilience, adventure, and pioneering spirit. As you journey through the destinations in this guide, pause to consider the historical significance of each place and how it has contributed to the vibrant mosaic that is Colorado today.

Front Range

1. Fort Collins

Nestled against the foothills of the Rocky Mountains, Fort Collins, Colorado, is a vibrant city known for its rich culture, outdoor recreation opportunities, and thriving craft beer scene. With a perfect blend of natural beauty and urban amenities, Fort Collins offers something for everyone, from hiking and biking to cultural events and culinary delights.

One of the city's main attractions is its extensive network of trails, perfect for hiking, mountain biking, and enjoying the great outdoors. Horsetooth Mountain Open Space, just west of the city, features miles of trails that wind through scenic landscapes of rugged rock formations and sweeping vistas of the foothills.

In addition to its outdoor recreation, Fort Collins boasts a lively arts and cultural scene. The city is home to numerous galleries, theaters, and music venues, showcasing local talent and attracting artists from around the region. Visitors can explore the Downtown Creative District, where they'll find an eclectic mix of shops, galleries, and restaurants housed in historic buildings.

No visit to Fort Collins would be complete without sampling some of its renowned craft beer. The city is often referred to as the "Napa Valley of Beer" due to its high concentration of breweries, including iconic names like New Belgium Brewing Company and Odell Brewing Company. Visitors can take brewery tours, participate in tastings, and learn about the art of craft brewing from the experts themselves.

For a taste of local history, visitors can explore the Fort Collins Museum of Discovery, which features interactive exhibits on science, history, and culture. The museum also offers educational programs and events for visitors of all ages.

2.   Celestial Seasonings Tea Factory

Located in Boulder, Colorado, the Celestial Seasonings Tea Factory offers visitors a fascinating journey through the world of tea. As one of the largest specialty tea manufacturers in North America, Celestial Seasonings has been delighting tea lovers with its flavorful blends for decades.

The factory tour begins with a walk through the Whimsical Tea Room, where visitors can sample a variety of Celestial Seasonings' most popular teas. From classic blends like Sleepytime and Chamomile to exotic flavors like Bengal Spice and Moroccan Pomegranate, there's something to suit every taste.

Next, visitors are taken behind the scenes to see how the magic happens. They'll witness the entire tea-making process, from blending and packaging to quality control and distribution. Along the way, they'll learn about the company's commitment to sustainability and environmental stewardship.

One of the highlights of the tour is the Mint Room, where visitors can experience the intense aroma of millions of pounds of peppermint and spearmint leaves. The room is kept at a chilly temperature to preserve the freshness of the mint, creating a truly unique sensory experience.

In addition to the factory tour, visitors can explore the Celestial Seasonings' headquarters, which features a charming gift shop where they can purchase their favorite teas and tea-related merchandise. The company also offers special events and tastings throughout the year, allowing visitors to further immerse themselves in the world of tea.

Whether you're a tea aficionado or simply curious about how tea is made, a visit to the Celestial Seasonings Tea Factory is sure to delight your senses and leave you with a newfound appreciation for this beloved beverage.

3. Boulder

Nestled against the majestic Rocky Mountains, Boulder, Colorado, is a vibrant city renowned for its stunning natural beauty, thriving arts scene, and innovative spirit. With its lively downtown, world-class restaurants, and endless outdoor recreation opportunities, Boulder offers a truly unique and unforgettable experience for visitors.

One of the city's most iconic attractions is the Flatirons, a series of distinctive rock formations that rise dramatically from the foothills just west of downtown. Visitors can hike, rock climb, or simply admire the breathtaking views of the Flatirons from one of the city's many parks and open spaces.

In addition to its natural beauty, Boulder is also known for its vibrant arts and culture scene. The city is home to numerous galleries, theaters, and music venues, showcasing local talent and attracting artists from around the world. Visitors can explore the vibrant Pearl Street Mall, where they'll find an eclectic mix of shops, restaurants, and street performers.

Boulder is also a hub of innovation and entrepreneurship, with a thriving tech industry and a strong focus on sustainability and environmental conservation. Visitors can tour the University of Colorado Boulder, which boasts world-class research facilities and a campus that is consistently ranked among the most beautiful in the country.

For foodies, Boulder offers a diverse culinary scene that reflects the city's commitment to fresh, locally sourced ingredients and innovative cuisine. From farm-to-table eateries to international fine dining, there's no shortage of delicious dining options to explore.

Whether you're seeking outdoor adventure, cultural enrichment, or simply a relaxing getaway, Boulder offers something for everyone. With its stunning natural landscapes, vibrant arts scene, and spirit of innovation, Boulder is truly a destination unlike any other.

4. Rocky Mountain Arsenal National Wildlife Refuge

Situated just northeast of Denver, Colorado, the Rocky Mountain Arsenal National Wildlife Refuge offers a peaceful retreat into nature, showcasing the region's diverse ecosystems and abundant wildlife. Once a site of industrial activity, the refuge has been transformed into a haven for native plants and animals, providing vital habitat for migratory birds, prairie mammals, and other wildlife species.

Visitors to the refuge can explore over 15,000 acres of restored prairie, wetlands, and woodlands, traversing a network of trails that wind through scenic landscapes of grassy meadows, shimmering lakes, and dense cottonwood groves. The refuge is home to a rich variety of wildlife, including bison, deer, coyotes, bald eagles, and over 330 species of birds, making it a paradise for birdwatchers and nature enthusiasts alike.

In addition to its natural beauty, the refuge also offers educational opportunities for visitors to learn about conservation, wildlife management, and the history of the area. The Visitor Center features interactive exhibits, interpretive displays, and educational programs that highlight the importance of preserving and protecting the region's natural resources.

Whether you're seeking solitude in nature, hoping to catch a glimpse of elusive wildlife, or simply looking for a scenic spot to explore, the Rocky Mountain Arsenal National Wildlife Refuge offers a tranquil escape from the hustle and bustle of city life, immersing visitors in the beauty and wonder of Colorado's natural landscapes.

5. Denver Museum of Nature & Science

Located in the heart of Denver's City Park, the Denver Museum of Nature & Science is a premier destination for science enthusiasts of all ages, offering a fascinating journey through the natural world and beyond. With its extensive collection of exhibits, interactive displays, and educational programs, the museum provides visitors with an opportunity to explore a wide range of scientific disciplines, from paleontology and anthropology to astronomy and biology.

One of the highlights of the museum is its impressive collection of dinosaur fossils, including a complete skeleton of a Tyrannosaurus rex, as well as specimens of triceratops, stegosaurus, and other prehistoric creatures. Visitors can marvel at these ancient fossils, learn about the process of fossilization, and even participate in a simulated dinosaur dig.

In addition to its dinosaur exhibits, the museum also features immersive displays on space exploration, human evolution, wildlife habitats, and more. Visitors can journey through the cosmos in the Gates Planetarium, explore the mysteries of ancient civilizations in the Egyptian Mummies exhibit, or get up close and personal with live insects in the Bug Brigade.

For families with children, the museum offers a variety of hands-on activities and educational programs designed to inspire curiosity and ignite a passion for science. From interactive experiments to guided tours, there's something for everyone to enjoy at the Denver Museum of Nature & Science.

Whether you're a science buff, a dinosaur enthusiast, or simply curious about the world around you, a visit to the Denver Museum of Nature & Science promises an unforgettable experience filled with wonder, discovery, and learning.

6.   City Park, Denver

City Park, located in the heart of Denver, Colorado, is a sprawling urban oasis that offers a tranquil retreat from the hustle and bustle of city life. Spanning 330 acres, the park features lush green spaces, scenic lakes, and majestic views of the Rocky Mountains, making it a beloved destination for locals and visitors alike.

One of the highlights of City Park is its picturesque lakes, where visitors can rent paddleboats, go fishing, or simply relax and enjoy the serene surroundings. The park's expansive lawns provide ample space for picnicking, playing sports, or soaking up the sun, while its winding pathways are perfect for walking, jogging, or biking.

In addition to its natural beauty, City Park also boasts several attractions and amenities for visitors to enjoy. The Denver Zoo, located within the park, is home to over 4,000 animals representing 600 species, making it a popular destination for families and animal lovers. The park is also home to the Denver Museum of Nature & Science, where visitors can explore exhibits on dinosaurs, space, wildlife, and more.

Throughout the year, City Park hosts a variety of events and festivals, including outdoor concerts, art fairs, and cultural celebrations. Visitors can experience the vibrant energy of the park as they stroll through its tree-lined pathways, take in the stunning views of the mountains, and immerse themselves in the sights and sounds of nature.

Whether you're seeking outdoor recreation, cultural enrichment, or simply a peaceful place to relax, City Park offers something for everyone, inviting visitors to escape the urban hustle and reconnect with the beauty and tranquility of nature.

7. Denver Zoo

The Denver Zoo, located in City Park, offers visitors an immersive and educational experience, showcasing a diverse array of wildlife from around the globe. With over 4,000 animals representing 600 species, the zoo provides a fascinating glimpse into the natural world and offers countless opportunities for learning, exploration, and conservation.

One of the highlights of the Denver Zoo is its innovative and immersive exhibits, which recreate natural habitats for the animals and provide visitors with an up-close look at their behavior and adaptations. From the lush rainforests of Tropical Discovery to the rugged terrain of Predator Ridge, each exhibit offers a unique and memorable experience, allowing visitors to connect with animals in a meaningful way.

In addition to its animal exhibits, the Denver Zoo also offers a variety of educational programs, presentations, and interactive experiences for visitors of all ages. From behind-the-scenes tours to animal encounters and keeper talks, there are plenty of opportunities to learn about wildlife conservation, animal behavior, and the importance of protecting endangered species.

For families with children, the zoo features a number of kid-friendly attractions, including a playground, a petting zoo, and a splash park, ensuring that visitors of all ages can enjoy a fun and memorable day at the zoo.

With its commitment to conservation, education, and animal welfare, the Denver Zoo is not only a top tourist destination but also a leader in wildlife conservation efforts, working to protect endangered species and their habitats both locally and globally. Whether you're a wildlife enthusiast, a nature lover, or simply looking for a fun and educational outing, the Denver Zoo offers an unforgettable adventure for visitors of all ages.

8.   Coors Field, Denver

Coors Field, located in the heart of downtown Denver, is a premier destination for baseball enthusiasts, offering an exciting and memorable experience for fans of America's favorite pastime. As the home stadium of the Colorado Rockies, Coors Field provides the perfect setting for cheering on the home team, enjoying the thrill of live baseball, and soaking up the vibrant atmosphere of game day.

One of the highlights of Coors Field is its stunning architecture and design, which blends modern amenities with classic ballpark charm. The stadium features breathtaking views of the Rocky Mountains, an expansive outfield plaza, and unique architectural elements inspired by the surrounding landscape, creating an iconic and unforgettable setting for baseball.

In addition to its picturesque setting, Coors Field also offers a wide range of amenities and attractions for fans to enjoy. From gourmet concessions and craft beer stands to interactive exhibits and children's play areas, there's something for everyone to enjoy at the ballpark.

For baseball purists, Coors Field offers a number of unique features and traditions, including the iconic "Rock Pile" section in center field, where fans can enjoy affordable tickets and panoramic views of the game. The stadium also hosts a variety of special events and promotions throughout the season, including fireworks nights, themed giveaways, and post-game concerts, ensuring that every visit to Coors Field is a memorable one.

Whether you're a die-hard baseball fan or simply looking for a fun and exciting outing with family and friends, Coors Field offers an unforgettable experience that celebrates the spirit of America's favorite pastime and brings people together in the heart of downtown Denver.

9.   Union Station, Denver

Union Station, located in the heart of downtown Denver, is a historic landmark and transportation hub that has been transformed into a vibrant and bustling destination for locals and visitors alike. With its stunning architecture, diverse dining options, and lively atmosphere, Union Station offers a unique blend of old-world charm and modern amenities, making it a popular gathering place for people of all ages.

Originally built in 1881, Union Station served as a bustling transportation hub for trains traveling across the country, connecting Denver to the rest of the nation. Today, the station has been beautifully restored and renovated, preserving its historic character while adding modern touches and amenities for today's travelers.

One of the highlights of Union Station is its stunning architecture and design, which features soaring ceilings, elegant archways, and intricate detailing throughout. Visitors can admire the station's grand interior spaces, including the iconic Great Hall, which serves as a welcoming gathering place for travelers and locals alike.

In addition to its historic charm, Union Station also offers a variety of dining options, ranging from casual cafes and grab-and-go eateries to upscale restaurants and cocktail bars. Visitors can enjoy a meal or a drink in one of the station's many dining venues, or simply relax and take in the bustling atmosphere of this iconic Denver landmark.

Union Station is also home to a number of shops, boutiques, and businesses, making it a popular destination for shopping, dining, and entertainment. Whether you're grabbing a cup of coffee, enjoying a leisurely meal, or simply people-watching in the Great Hall, Union Station offers a one-of-a-kind experience that celebrates the rich history and vibrant culture of Denver.

10. Downtown Aquarium, Denver

The Downtown Aquarium in Denver offers visitors a unique and immersive experience, inviting them to explore the wonders of the ocean without ever leaving land. Situated in the heart of downtown Denver, this expansive aquarium features a variety of exhibits and attractions that showcase marine life from around the world, making it a must-visit destination for families, animal lovers, and aquarium enthusiasts alike.

One of the highlights of the Downtown Aquarium is its impressive collection of marine animals, including sharks, stingrays, sea turtles, and colorful tropical fish. Visitors can stroll through the aquarium's underwater tunnels, where they'll be surrounded by sharks and other marine creatures swimming overhead, providing a thrilling and unforgettable experience.

In addition to its animal exhibits, the Downtown Aquarium also offers a variety of interactive experiences and educational programs for visitors of all ages. From touch tanks and feeding sessions to behind-the-scenes tours and educational presentations, there are plenty of opportunities to learn about marine life and conservation while having fun at the same time.

For families with children, the aquarium features a number of kid-friendly attractions, including a 4-D theater, a playground, and a carousel, ensuring that young visitors are entertained and engaged throughout their visit. The aquarium also offers birthday party packages, summer camps, and other special events, making it a popular destination for families celebrating special occasions.

Whether you're marveling at the beauty of a coral reef, getting up close and personal with a sea turtle, or learning about the importance of protecting our oceans, the Downtown Aquarium offers a truly immersive and educational experience that delights visitors of all ages and backgrounds.

11. 16th Street Mall, Denver

The 16th Street Mall in Denver is a bustling pedestrian promenade that stretches for over a mile through the heart of downtown, offering visitors a vibrant and eclectic mix of shops, restaurants, entertainment venues, and cultural attractions. With its lively atmosphere, stunning architecture, and unique blend of local and national retailers, the 16th Street Mall is a must-visit destination for tourists and locals alike.

One of the highlights of the 16th Street Mall is its wide array of shopping options, ranging from high-end boutiques and specialty stores to national chains and souvenir shops. Visitors can browse for everything from clothing and accessories to jewelry, artwork, and Colorado-themed gifts, making it the perfect place to find that one-of-a-kind souvenir or gift for loved ones back home.

In addition to its shopping opportunities, the 16th Street Mall also offers a variety of dining options to suit every palate and budget. Visitors can choose from a diverse array of restaurants, cafes, and eateries, ranging from upscale dining establishments and gourmet food trucks to casual bistros and fast-casual chains. Whether you're craving pizza, sushi, barbecue, or international cuisine, you'll find plenty of delicious options to satisfy your appetite.

Beyond shopping and dining, the 16th Street Mall also offers a variety of entertainment options, including theaters, art galleries, and live music venues. Visitors can catch a movie at the Denver Pavilions, take in a performance at the Denver Center for the Performing Arts, or simply enjoy the vibrant street performers and musicians who entertain crowds along the mall.

Whether you're looking to shop 'til you drop, dine al fresco, or simply soak up the sights and sounds of downtown Denver, the 16th Street Mall offers an unforgettable experience that captures the essence of the city's vibrant culture and energy.

12. Denver Performing Arts Complex

The Denver Performing Arts Complex, located in the heart of downtown Denver, is a premier destination for theatergoers, music lovers, and performing arts enthusiasts, offering a diverse array of world-class performances and cultural experiences. As one of the largest performing arts centers in the country, the complex is home to a variety of theaters, concert halls, and performance spaces, each showcasing the best in theater, dance, opera, and music.

One of the highlights of the Denver Performing Arts Complex is its impressive lineup of performances, which includes Broadway musicals, opera productions, ballet performances, symphony concerts, and more. Visitors can catch a show at one of the complex's many venues, including the Ellie Caulkins Opera House, the Buell Theatre, and Boettcher Concert Hall, each offering a unique and memorable experience.

In addition to its performances, the Denver Performing Arts Complex also offers a variety of educational programs, workshops, and outreach initiatives designed to engage audiences of all ages and backgrounds. From student matinees and artist residencies to community partnerships and youth programs, the complex is committed to fostering a love of the arts and ensuring that everyone has access to high-quality cultural experiences.

For visitors looking to explore the complex further, guided tours are available, offering behind-the-scenes access to the theaters, rehearsal spaces, and production facilities. Visitors can learn about the history and architecture of the complex, as well as the artists, performers, and productions that have graced its stages over the years.

Whether you're attending a world-class performance, exploring the complex on a guided tour, or simply soaking up the vibrant atmosphere of downtown Denver, the Denver Performing Arts Complex offers an unforgettable experience that celebrates the power of creativity, imagination, and artistic expression.

13. Denver Mint

The Denver Mint, one of the United States Mint facilities, stands as a testament to the nation's monetary history and the art of coin production. Located in downtown Denver, Colorado, the Denver Mint offers visitors a fascinating glimpse into the process of minting coins and the rich heritage of American currency.

As one of the oldest federal institutions in the Rocky Mountain region, the Denver Mint has been producing coins since 1906. Visitors to the mint can embark on guided tours that take them through the various stages of coin production, from the initial design and engraving process to the striking of coins and their distribution into circulation.

One of the highlights of the tour is the opportunity to witness the coin production floor, where state-of-the-art machinery and skilled craftsmen work together to create millions of coins each day. Visitors can observe the intricate process of blanking, annealing, and striking coins, as well as learn about the history and significance of different coin designs and denominations.

In addition to its role in coin production, the Denver Mint also houses a museum that showcases the history of the mint and its contributions to American numismatics. Visitors can explore exhibits on the mint's founding, its role in supporting the nation's economy, and its impact on the development of American currency over the years.

For coin collectors and history enthusiasts, a visit to the Denver Mint offers a unique and educational experience that celebrates the artistry, innovation, and tradition of coin production in the United States.

14. Denver Art Museum

The Denver Art Museum (DAM) stands as a cultural centerpiece in the heart of Denver, Colorado, offering visitors a diverse array of artistic treasures from around the world. With its striking architecture, extensive collection, and dynamic exhibitions, the museum provides an enriching and immersive experience that celebrates the beauty, diversity, and creativity of human expression.

One of the highlights of the Denver Art Museum is its vast collection of American Indian art, which includes thousands of works representing Native American cultures from across North America. Visitors can explore galleries devoted to traditional and contemporary art, as well as artifacts, textiles, and decorative objects that showcase the rich heritage and artistic traditions of indigenous peoples.

In addition to its American Indian art, the museum also boasts impressive collections of European, Asian, African, and modern and contemporary art, featuring masterpieces by renowned artists such as Claude Monet, Vincent van Gogh, Georgia O'Keeffe, and Andy Warhol. Visitors can admire paintings, sculptures, ceramics, and other works of art that span thousands of years and cultures, offering a comprehensive survey of human creativity and expression.

In addition to its permanent collections, the Denver Art Museum also hosts a variety of temporary exhibitions, special events, and educational programs throughout the year, ensuring that there's always something new and exciting to discover. Whether you're a seasoned art enthusiast or simply looking to explore the world of art and culture, a visit to the Denver Art Museum promises an unforgettable experience that inspires, educates, and delights visitors of all ages.

15. Colorado State Capitol Building

The Colorado State Capitol Building, located in downtown Denver, is a historic landmark and architectural masterpiece that serves as the seat of government for the state of Colorado. Designed by architect Elijah E. Myers and completed in 1894, the capitol building stands as a symbol of democracy, freedom, and the rich history of the Centennial State.

One of the most striking features of the Colorado State Capitol is its magnificent gold dome, which rises 272 feet above the city skyline and is adorned with real gold leaf. The dome is topped by a statue of a Native American woman, known as the "Gold State of Colorado," which symbolizes the state's mining heritage and its pioneering spirit.

Visitors to the capitol can take guided tours that provide insight into the building's history, architecture, and significance. Highlights of the tour include the ornate interior spaces, such as the grand staircase, the House and Senate chambers, and the historic Supreme Court chamber, which feature intricate woodwork, stained glass windows, and decorative murals that showcase the craftsmanship and artistry of the era.

In addition to its architectural beauty, the Colorado State Capitol also houses a variety of historical artifacts, including portraits, sculptures, and memorabilia that commemorate the state's rich heritage and its role in shaping the American West. Visitors can learn about Colorado's colorful history, from its frontier days and mining boom to its role in the women's suffrage movement and its modern-day political landscape.

For those interested in politics and government, the Colorado State Capitol offers a unique opportunity to witness democracy in action. Visitors can observe legislative sessions, committee hearings, and other civic activities, as well as interact with state lawmakers and officials who work to shape the future of Colorado.

Whether you're interested in history, architecture, or politics, a visit to the Colorado State Capitol Building offers a fascinating and educational experience that celebrates the spirit of democracy and the rich heritage of the Centennial State.

16. Denver Botanic Gardens

The Denver Botanic Gardens is a tranquil haven located in the heart of Denver, Colorado, offering visitors a delightful escape into the world of plants, flowers, and natural beauty. Spanning 24 acres, the botanic gardens feature a diverse array of themed gardens, immersive exhibits, and educational programs that celebrate the rich diversity of plant life from around the globe.

One of the highlights of the Denver Botanic Gardens is its stunning collection of gardens, each meticulously designed to showcase different plant species and ecosystems. Visitors can stroll through lush landscapes such as the Japanese Garden, the Rock Alpine Garden, and the Romantic Gardens, marveling at the vibrant colors, fragrant blooms, and intricate designs that fill each space.

In addition to its gardens, the botanic gardens also feature a variety of exhibits and attractions that highlight the importance of plants in our lives and the natural world. Visitors can explore interactive exhibits on topics such as ecology, conservation, and sustainability, as well as attend workshops, lectures, and special events that offer insight into gardening, horticulture, and botany.

For families with children, the Denver Botanic Gardens offers a number of kid-friendly activities and attractions, including a children's garden, a nature play area, and educational programs designed to inspire a love of nature and gardening at a young age.

Whether you're a plant enthusiast, a nature lover, or simply looking for a peaceful retreat from the hustle and bustle of city life, the Denver Botanic Gardens offers a serene and enchanting experience that nourishes the mind, body, and soul.

17. Red Rocks Park and Amphitheatre

Red Rocks Park and Amphitheatre, located just west of Denver in Morrison, Colorado, is a geological wonder and world-renowned music venue that offers visitors a unique and unforgettable experience. Carved out of ancient sandstone, the natural amphitheater is surrounded by towering red rock formations that create acoustics unlike any other, making it a favorite destination for musicians and concertgoers alike.

One of the highlights of Red Rocks Park is its stunning natural beauty, which provides a picturesque backdrop for outdoor recreation and relaxation. Visitors can hike, bike, or horseback ride through the park's miles of trails, taking in breathtaking views of the surrounding foothills and valleys, or simply enjoy a leisurely picnic amidst the towering rock formations.

In addition to its natural attractions, Red Rocks Park is also home to the iconic Red Rocks Amphitheatre, a legendary music venue that has hosted some of the biggest names in music since its opening in 1941. Concertgoers can attend live performances by world-class artists and bands, surrounded by the majestic beauty of the Colorado landscape and the natural acoustics of the amphitheater.

For those interested in the park's history and geology, guided tours are available that provide insight into the formation of the red rock formations, as well as the cultural significance of the amphitheater and its role in the music industry.

Whether you're attending a concert under the stars, exploring the park's scenic trails, or simply marveling at the beauty of nature's handiwork, Red Rocks Park and Amphitheatre offers a truly magical and memorable experience that captivates visitors of all ages and interests.

18. Cherry Creek State Park

Cherry Creek State Park, located in Aurora, Colorado, just southeast of downtown Denver, offers visitors a peaceful retreat into nature amidst the bustling city. Spanning over 4,000 acres, the park features a pristine reservoir, scenic trails, and abundant wildlife, making it a popular destination for outdoor recreation and relaxation.

One of the highlights of Cherry Creek State Park is its expansive reservoir, which offers a variety of water-based activities for visitors to enjoy. Boating, fishing, and swimming are popular pastimes on the reservoir, and visitors can rent kayaks, paddleboards, and other watercraft from the park's marina or swim at the designated swim beach.

In addition to its water-based activities, Cherry Creek State Park offers a network of trails that wind through diverse ecosystems, including wetlands, grasslands, and woodlands. Hikers, bikers, and horseback riders can explore miles of scenic trails that offer stunning views of the reservoir and surrounding landscapes, as well as opportunities to spot wildlife such as deer, rabbits, and migratory birds.

For families with children, the park features a variety of amenities and attractions, including picnic areas, playgrounds, and nature programs that offer hands-on learning experiences and outdoor adventures for kids of all ages.

Whether you're seeking outdoor adventure, relaxation, or simply a break from the hustle and bustle of city life, Cherry Creek State Park offers a natural oasis in the heart of the city that invites visitors to connect with nature, recharge their spirits, and create lasting memories amidst the beauty of Colorado's great outdoors.

19. United States Air Force Academy

The United States Air Force Academy, located in Colorado Springs, Colorado, stands as a symbol of excellence in leadership, education, and military training. Founded in 1954, the academy serves as the premier institution for preparing young men and women to become officers in the United States Air Force, fostering a culture of academic rigor, physical fitness, and moral integrity.

One of the highlights of the United States Air Force Academy is its stunning campus, which spans over 18,000 acres of pristine Colorado landscape, nestled against the backdrop of the Rocky Mountains. Visitors to the academy can explore its impressive facilities, including the iconic Cadet Chapel, which features soaring spires and stunning stained glass windows that symbolize the academy's commitment to faith, character, and service.

In addition to its architectural landmarks, the United States Air Force Academy offers a variety of educational programs, military training, and extracurricular activities for cadets. Visitors can attend lectures, demonstrations, and sporting events, or participate in guided tours that provide insight into the academy's rigorous academic curriculum, leadership development programs, and military training exercises.

For those interested in the academy's history and heritage, the Barry Goldwater Visitor Center offers exhibits, displays, and interactive experiences that highlight the academy's proud traditions, distinguished alumni, and contributions to national security.

Whether you're a prospective cadet, a military history buff, or simply curious about the training and education of future Air Force officers, a visit to the United States Air Force Academy offers a unique and inspiring experience that celebrates the values of courage, integrity, and excellence that define the United States Air Force.

20. Garden of the Gods

The Garden of the Gods, located in Colorado Springs, Colorado, is a breathtaking natural wonder that showcases the majestic beauty of the Rocky Mountains and the intricate artistry of geological formations. Designated as a National Natural Landmark, the Garden of the Gods spans over 1,300 acres of red rock spires, towering sandstone formations, and lush green valleys, making it a popular destination for outdoor enthusiasts, nature lovers, and photographers.

One of the highlights of the Garden of the Gods is its iconic rock formations, which rise dramatically from the earth, sculpted over millions of years by the forces of wind, water, and time. Visitors can explore the park's network of hiking trails, bike paths, and scenic overlooks, marveling at the stunning vistas of Pikes Peak and the surrounding landscape.

In addition to its natural beauty, the Garden of the Gods also offers a variety of recreational activities for visitors to enjoy, including rock climbing, horseback riding, and nature walks. The park's Visitor and Nature Center features exhibits, interpretive displays, and guided tours that provide insight into the geology, ecology, and cultural history of the area.

Whether you're hiking among towering rock formations, picnicking in a scenic valley, or simply soaking up the beauty of nature, a visit to the Garden of the Gods offers an unforgettable experience that celebrates the wonders of the natural world and inspires a sense of awe and wonder.

21. Manitou Springs

Nestled at the foot of Pikes Peak, Manitou Springs is a charming mountain town located just west of Colorado Springs, Colorado, offering visitors a delightful blend of natural beauty, historic charm, and quirky attractions. With its colorful Victorian architecture, eclectic shops, and natural mineral springs, Manitou Springs has long been a beloved destination for travelers seeking adventure, relaxation, and rejuvenation.

One of the highlights of Manitou Springs is its natural mineral springs, which flow from underground aquifers and are renowned for their therapeutic properties. Visitors can stroll along the town's charming streets and sample the mineral-rich waters from a variety of public fountains and springs, or indulge in a soak at one of the area's historic mineral spas.

In addition to its natural springs, Manitou Springs offers a variety of attractions and activities for visitors to enjoy, including art galleries, boutique shops, and local restaurants serving up delicious cuisine and craft beverages. The town also hosts a variety of festivals, events, and live music performances throughout the year, celebrating its rich cultural heritage and vibrant arts scene.

For outdoor enthusiasts, Manitou Springs serves as a gateway to the Pikes Peak region, offering access to a variety of hiking, biking, and outdoor recreation opportunities. Visitors can explore nearby trails, parks, and scenic overlooks, or embark on a scenic drive to the summit of Pikes Peak, where they'll be rewarded with breathtaking views of the surrounding mountains and valleys.

Whether you're seeking relaxation, adventure, or simply a charming mountain town to explore, Manitou Springs offers a warm welcome and a unique blend of natural beauty, historic charm, and quirky attractions that captivate visitors of all ages and interests.

22. Colorado Springs

Nestled at the base of the majestic Rocky Mountains, Colorado Springs is a vibrant city that offers a perfect blend of natural beauty, outdoor adventure, and cultural attractions. Known for its stunning landscapes, diverse recreational opportunities, and thriving arts scene, Colorado Springs attracts visitors from around the world who come to explore its scenic wonders and experience its unique charm.

One of the highlights of Colorado Springs is its abundance of outdoor recreation opportunities. With over 300 days of sunshine each year, the city boasts miles of hiking and biking trails, world-class rock climbing spots, and scenic parks where visitors can enjoy activities such as picnicking, fishing, and wildlife watching. Iconic attractions like Garden of the Gods, Pikes Peak, and Seven Falls showcase the city's natural splendor and provide endless opportunities for adventure and exploration.

In addition to its outdoor attractions, Colorado Springs is home to a vibrant arts and cultural scene. Visitors can explore galleries, museums, and performance venues throughout the city, discovering local art, history, and culture along the way. From the Colorado Springs Fine Arts Center to the Colorado Springs Pioneers Museum, there's always something new and exciting to experience in the city's thriving arts community.

For those seeking a taste of history and heritage, Colorado Springs offers a wealth of historic sites and landmarks to explore. The city's rich past is reflected in its historic neighborhoods, charming downtown area, and iconic landmarks such as the United States Air Force Academy, the Broadmoor Hotel, and the Colorado Springs Pioneers Museum.

Whether you're an outdoor enthusiast, a culture buff, or simply looking for a scenic escape, Colorado Springs offers something for everyone. With its stunning landscapes, vibrant arts scene, and rich cultural heritage, the city invites visitors to discover the endless possibilities for adventure and exploration in the heart of the Rocky Mountains.

23. Sand Creek Library

The Sand Creek Library, located in Colorado Springs, serves as a vital community hub for learning, enrichment, and connection. As part of the Pikes Peak Library District, the library provides access to a wide range of resources, programs, and services that support lifelong learning and foster a sense of community among residents of all ages.

One of the highlights of the Sand Creek Library is its extensive collection of books, audiobooks, DVDs, and digital resources that cater to diverse interests and learning styles. From bestsellers and classics to educational materials and children's literature, the library's collection offers something for everyone, making it a valuable resource for residents seeking information, entertainment, or inspiration.

In addition to its collection, the Sand Creek Library offers a variety of programs and services designed to engage and empower members of the community. From storytime sessions and book clubs to computer classes and job search assistance, the library provides opportunities for learning, skill-building, and personal growth that enrich the lives of its patrons.

For families with children, the Sand Creek Library offers a dedicated children's area with age-appropriate books, games, and activities that encourage early literacy and lifelong learning. The library also hosts special events and programs for children and families throughout the year, including author visits, craft workshops, and summer reading challenges.

Beyond its role as a repository of knowledge and information, the Sand Creek Library serves as a gathering place where residents can connect with one another, share ideas, and build community. Whether attending a community meeting, participating in a discussion group, or simply browsing the shelves, visitors to the library are welcomed with open arms and encouraged to explore, learn, and grow together.

24. Fort Carson

Fort Carson, located just south of Colorado Springs, has played a significant role in the military history and heritage of the Pikes Peak region for over 75 years. As home to the 4th Infantry Division and numerous other military units, Fort Carson serves as a vital training and deployment center for the United States Army, as well as a valued member of the Colorado Springs community.

One of the highlights of Fort Carson is its commitment to readiness and excellence in training. The base offers state-of-the-art facilities and resources to support the training and development of soldiers, including live-fire ranges, simulation centers, and obstacle courses that simulate real-world combat scenarios. Soldiers undergo rigorous training in combat skills, leadership, and teamwork, ensuring that they are prepared to meet the challenges of today's military missions.

In addition to its training mission, Fort Carson is also actively involved in supporting the local community and building partnerships with civic organizations, businesses, and educational institutions. The base participates in a variety of community outreach programs, volunteer initiatives, and public events that promote goodwill and strengthen ties between the military and civilian populations.

For military personnel and their families stationed at Fort Carson, the base offers a wide range of amenities and support services to enhance quality of life and promote well-being. From recreational facilities and family housing to medical services and educational opportunities, Fort Carson strives to create a supportive and welcoming environment for service members and their loved ones.

Whether training soldiers for deployment, supporting the local community, or providing essential services to military families, Fort Carson stands as a proud symbol of the United States Army's commitment to service, sacrifice, and excellence in the Pikes Peak region and beyond.

25. Cheyenne Mountain Zoo

Perched atop Cheyenne Mountain in Colorado Springs, the Cheyenne Mountain Zoo is not just your average zoo – it's a conservation haven and educational paradise. Founded in 1926, this mountain zoo holds the prestigious title of being the only zoo in the United States located on a mountainside, providing visitors with breathtaking views and unforgettable experiences.

One of the highlights of Cheyenne Mountain Zoo is its commitment to conservation and animal welfare. The zoo participates in numerous breeding programs for endangered species, including the black-footed ferret and the Wyoming toad, helping to ensure the survival of these animals for future generations. Visitors can witness these conservation efforts firsthand through interactive exhibits and educational programs that highlight the importance of protecting wildlife and their habitats.

In addition to its conservation efforts, Cheyenne Mountain Zoo offers a wide array of animal exhibits and attractions that showcase the diversity of life on Earth. From African elephants and giraffes to grizzly bears and red pandas, the zoo is home to over 750 animals representing more than 170 species from around the world. Visitors can get up close and personal with these animals through feeding experiences, keeper talks, and animal encounters that provide insight into their behavior, biology, and conservation status.

For families with children, Cheyenne Mountain Zoo offers a variety of kid-friendly attractions and activities, including a petting zoo, carousel, and play area. The zoo also hosts special events and programs throughout the year, such as Boo at the Zoo and Electric Safari, which provide opportunities for families to connect with animals and nature in fun and interactive ways.

Whether you're a wildlife enthusiast, a nature lover, or simply looking for a fun and educational outing with family and friends, Cheyenne Mountain Zoo offers an unforgettable experience that celebrates the beauty and diversity of the natural world while inspiring a sense of stewardship and conservation in its visitors.

26. Pikes Peak

Standing tall at 14,115 feet above sea level, Pikes Peak is an iconic landmark and outdoor playground that looms over the city of Colorado Springs. Known as "America's Mountain," Pikes Peak offers visitors a stunning alpine landscape, breathtaking views, and endless opportunities for outdoor adventure and exploration.

One of the highlights of Pikes Peak is its accessibility. Visitors can reach the summit of the mountain by driving the scenic Pikes Peak Highway, which winds its way through rugged terrain and towering forests to the summit. Along the way, travelers can stop at scenic overlooks, picnic areas, and interpretive sites that provide information about the history, geology, and ecology of the mountain.

For those seeking a more adventurous experience, Pikes Peak offers a variety of hiking trails that range from easy walks to challenging climbs. Popular routes include the Barr Trail, which leads hikers to the summit of the mountain, and the Crags Trail, which offers stunning views of the surrounding landscape. Whether you're a seasoned hiker or a casual nature lover, there's a trail on Pikes Peak for everyone to enjoy.

In addition to its hiking trails, Pikes Peak also offers opportunities for fishing, camping, and wildlife viewing in its surrounding forests and meadows. Visitors can explore the mountain's diverse ecosystems, spotting wildlife such as elk, mule deer, and bighorn sheep, or simply take in the beauty of the alpine landscape.

Whether you're driving to the summit, hiking a scenic trail, or simply admiring the view from afar, a visit to Pikes Peak offers an unforgettable experience that celebrates the beauty and majesty of Colorado's Rocky Mountains. With its stunning vistas, outdoor recreation opportunities, and rich natural history, Pikes Peak truly lives up to its reputation as "America's Mountain."

Front Range Map 1 – Destinations 1-4

Front Range Map 2 – Destinations 5-15

Front Range Map 3 – Destinations 17-18

Front Range Map 4 – Destinations 19-26

Eastern Plains

1.   Pawnee Buttes

Located in the northeastern corner of Colorado, the Pawnee Buttes stand as a striking geological formation rising from the vast expanse of the Great Plains. These iconic buttes, sculpted by millennia of erosion, offer visitors a glimpse into the region's rich natural history and provide opportunities for hiking, wildlife viewing, and photography.

One of the highlights of the Pawnee Buttes is their unique geological features, which include towering sandstone cliffs, rugged canyons, and expansive prairie vistas. Visitors can explore the area's trails, which wind through grasslands and sagebrush, offering opportunities to spot wildlife such as pronghorn antelope, mule deer, and prairie dogs. Birdwatchers will also delight in the chance to see a variety of bird species, including raptors, songbirds, and migratory birds.

In addition to its natural beauty, the Pawnee Buttes hold cultural significance for Native American tribes, who consider the area to be sacred ground. Visitors can learn about the history and heritage of the region through interpretive signs and displays that highlight the cultural and ecological importance of the buttes to indigenous peoples.

For those seeking outdoor adventure, the Pawnee Buttes offer opportunities for hiking, camping, and photography. The area's remote location and dark skies also make it an ideal spot for stargazing, providing visitors with a chance to marvel at the wonders of the night sky far from the lights of the city.

Whether you're exploring the trails, spotting wildlife, or simply taking in the beauty of the Colorado plains, a visit to the Pawnee Buttes offers a unique and unforgettable experience that celebrates the natural wonders of the Great Plains.

2.   Crow Valley Recreation Area

Tucked away in the northeastern corner of Colorado, the Crow Valley Recreation Area offers visitors a tranquil escape into nature amidst the rolling hills and prairie grasslands of the High Plains. With its scenic beauty, diverse wildlife, and opportunities for outdoor recreation, Crow Valley is a hidden gem waiting to be discovered by outdoor enthusiasts and nature lovers alike.

One of the highlights of the Crow Valley Recreation Area is its pristine natural landscape, which provides habitat for a variety of plant and animal species. Visitors can explore the area's hiking trails, which wind through grasslands, wetlands, and riparian habitats, offering opportunities to spot wildlife such as deer, elk, coyotes, and migratory birds.

In addition to its natural beauty, Crow Valley also offers a variety of recreational activities for visitors to enjoy. Anglers can cast a line in the area's ponds and streams, which are stocked with trout, bass, and other game fish, while birdwatchers can observe a variety of bird species, including waterfowl, shorebirds, and songbirds.

For those seeking a longer stay, Crow Valley offers camping facilities with tent and RV sites, as well as picnic areas and group shelters for day use. Whether you're enjoying a leisurely hike, casting a line in the water, or simply relaxing amidst the beauty of nature, Crow Valley offers a peaceful and rejuvenating retreat from the hustle and bustle of everyday life.

Whether you're exploring the trails, birdwatching by the ponds, or simply soaking in the serenity of the Colorado landscape, a visit to Crow Valley Recreation Area promises an unforgettable experience that celebrates the beauty and diversity of the High Plains.

3. Kit Carson County Carousel

Located in Burlington, Colorado, the Kit Carson County Carousel is a beloved landmark and cultural treasure that delights visitors of all ages with its whimsical charm and rich history. Built in 1905 by the Philadelphia Toboggan Company, this historic carousel is one of the few remaining antique wooden carousels in the country and is listed on the National Register of Historic Places.

One of the highlights of the Kit Carson County Carousel is its stunning craftsmanship and intricate design. The carousel features 46 hand-carved wooden animals, including horses, lions, tigers, and bears, as well as two chariots adorned with colorful paintings and decorative elements. Each animal is a unique work of art, with its own distinctive features and personality, making every ride on the carousel a magical experience.

In addition to its beautiful craftsmanship, the Kit Carson County Carousel holds special significance for the community of Burlington and the surrounding area. Generations of families have enjoyed rides on the carousel, creating cherished memories that have been passed down through the years. Visitors can learn about the carousel's history and heritage through interpretive displays and guided tours, which provide insight into its construction, restoration, and ongoing preservation efforts.

For those seeking a nostalgic trip back in time, the Kit Carson County Carousel offers a delightful ride through history that celebrates the joy and wonder of childhood. Whether you're riding the carousel for the first time or reliving cherished memories from years past, a visit to this historic landmark promises an enchanting experience that captures the imagination and delights the senses.

4. Sand Creek Massacre National Historic Site

The Sand Creek Massacre National Historic Site, located in southeastern Colorado near the town of Eads, serves as a solemn reminder of one of the darkest chapters in American history. This site commemorates the tragic events that unfolded on November 29, 1864, when a peaceful encampment of Cheyenne and Arapaho Indians was brutally attacked by United States cavalry forces, resulting in the deaths of hundreds of men, women, and children.

One of the highlights of the Sand Creek Massacre National Historic Site is its historical significance, which sheds light on the complex and often violent interactions between Native American tribes and European settlers during the westward expansion of the United States. Visitors can explore the site's interpretive center, which features exhibits, artifacts, and multimedia presentations that provide insight into the events leading up to the massacre, as well as its aftermath and legacy.

In addition to its historical exhibits, the Sand Creek Massacre National Historic Site offers opportunities for reflection and remembrance. Visitors can walk the site's trails, which wind through the grassy plains and along the banks of Sand Creek, where the massacre took place. Interpretive signs and markers along the way provide context and perspective, allowing visitors to learn about the lives of the Cheyenne and Arapaho people who were affected by the tragedy.

For those seeking to honor the memory of the victims and learn from the mistakes of the past, the Sand Creek Massacre National Historic Site offers a powerful and poignant experience that encourages reflection, empathy, and understanding. By preserving this important piece of American history, the site serves as a testament to the resilience of Native American communities and a reminder of the ongoing struggle for justice and reconciliation.

5. Lamar Community College Library and Cultural Center

The Lamar Community College Library and Cultural Center, located in Lamar, Colorado, serves as a vibrant hub of learning, innovation, and creativity for students, faculty, and community members alike. With its extensive collection of resources, state-of-the-art facilities, and dynamic programming, the library plays a vital role in supporting academic success, promoting cultural enrichment, and fostering lifelong learning in the Lamar community.

One of the highlights of the Lamar Community College Library and Cultural Center is its comprehensive collection of books, periodicals, digital resources, and multimedia materials that cater to diverse interests and learning needs. From academic textbooks and research journals to popular fiction and children's literature, the library offers something for everyone, making it a valuable resource for students, scholars, and lifelong learners alike.

In addition to its collection, the Lamar Community College Library and Cultural Center offers a variety of programs and services designed to engage and inspire members of the community. Visitors can attend author talks, book readings, and cultural events, or participate in workshops, seminars, and educational programs that promote literacy, creativity, and lifelong learning. The library also hosts art exhibitions, film screenings, and performances that showcase the talents of local artists and performers, enriching the cultural life of the Lamar community.

For students and faculty at Lamar Community College, the library serves as a hub of academic support and resources, providing access to research assistance, tutoring services, and study spaces that enhance the learning experience. Whether you're conducting research for a class project, exploring new ideas and interests, or simply looking for a quiet place to study, the Lamar Community College Library and Cultural Center offers a welcoming and supportive environment that fosters intellectual growth, personal development, and community engagement.

6. John Martin Dam

John Martin Dam, situated on the Arkansas River in southeastern Colorado near the town of Las Animas, is an impressive feat of engineering that serves as a vital component of the region's water management infrastructure. Completed in 1948 by the United States Army Corps of Engineers, the dam plays a crucial role in flood control, irrigation, and hydroelectric power generation, while also providing recreational opportunities for visitors to enjoy.

One of the highlights of John Martin Dam is its sheer size and scale. Standing at over 130 feet tall and stretching more than 3,000 feet across the Arkansas River, the dam creates John Martin Reservoir, a massive body of water that spans over 8,000 acres and serves as a valuable water source for agricultural, municipal, and industrial purposes throughout the region.

In addition to its practical functions, John Martin Dam also offers recreational opportunities for outdoor enthusiasts and nature lovers to enjoy. The reservoir provides excellent fishing, boating, and water-based recreation, with anglers casting lines in search of catfish, walleye, bass, and other game fish. Boaters can explore the reservoir's calm waters by kayak, canoe, or motorboat, while birdwatchers and wildlife enthusiasts can spot a variety of bird species and wildlife along the reservoir's shores and surrounding wetlands.

For those interested in learning more about the dam's history and engineering, John Martin Dam offers guided tours, interpretive displays, and educational programs that provide insight into its construction, operation, and ongoing maintenance. Visitors can explore the dam's visitor center, which features exhibits on topics such as water management, hydroelectric power generation, and the environmental impact of dams on river ecosystems.

Whether you're enjoying a day of fishing on the reservoir, exploring the surrounding wetlands, or learning about the dam's engineering and history, John Martin Dam offers a unique and educational experience that celebrates the importance of water management and conservation in the arid landscapes of southeastern Colorado.

7. John Martin Reservoir State Park

Located in southeastern Colorado near the town of Las Animas, John Martin Reservoir State Park offers visitors a peaceful retreat amidst the scenic beauty of the Arkansas River Valley. With its sprawling reservoir, diverse wildlife habitats, and opportunities for outdoor recreation, the park provides a haven for nature lovers, anglers, and outdoor enthusiasts of all ages.

One of the highlights of John Martin Reservoir State Park is its expansive reservoir, which spans over 8,000 acres and offers ample opportunities for boating, fishing, and water-based recreation. Anglers can cast a line in search of catfish, walleye, bass, and other game fish, while boaters can explore the reservoir's calm waters by kayak, canoe, or motorboat. The park also features several boat ramps, marinas, and fishing piers that provide convenient access to the water for visitors of all skill levels.

In addition to its water-based activities, John Martin Reservoir State Park offers a variety of recreational opportunities on land. Visitors can explore the park's network of hiking and biking trails, which wind through scenic landscapes such as wetlands, grasslands, and cottonwood groves, providing opportunities to spot wildlife such as deer, coyotes, and migratory birds. Picnic areas, campgrounds, and group shelters are also available for those looking to enjoy a leisurely day in the great outdoors.

For birdwatchers and nature enthusiasts, John Martin Reservoir State Park is a prime destination for spotting a variety of bird species, including waterfowl, shorebirds, and raptors. The park's diverse habitats provide important nesting and feeding grounds for birds migrating along the Central Flyway, making it a popular spot for birdwatching and wildlife photography throughout the year.

Whether you're boating on the reservoir, hiking through the scenic landscapes, or simply enjoying a picnic with family and friends, John Martin Reservoir State Park offers a tranquil and rejuvenating escape that celebrates the beauty and diversity of Colorado's natural landscapes. With its abundant recreational opportunities and scenic beauty, the park invites visitors to connect with nature, relax, and unwind amidst the peaceful surroundings of the Arkansas River Valley.

8. Picketwire Valley

Picketwire Valley, located in southeastern Colorado near the town of La Junta, offers visitors a journey through time and history, with its rich cultural heritage and archaeological significance. Named after the Purgatoire River, which flows through the valley, Picketwire Valley is home to a variety of historical sites and landmarks that provide insight into the region's Native American, Hispanic, and pioneer heritage.

One of the highlights of Picketwire Valley is its wealth of archaeological sites and petroglyphs, which date back thousands of years and offer clues to the area's prehistoric past. Visitors can explore rock art panels, ancient dwellings, and other archaeological sites that provide a glimpse into the lives and cultures of the Native American tribes who inhabited the valley long before European settlers arrived.

In addition to its archaeological sites, Picketwire Valley also features a variety of historical landmarks and points of interest related to the region's Hispanic and pioneer heritage. Visitors can visit historic ranches, adobe buildings, and old homesteads that tell the story of the valley's settlement and development by Hispanic settlers and early pioneers.

For those interested in exploring the natural beauty of Picketwire Valley, the area offers opportunities for hiking, birdwatching, and wildlife viewing amidst its scenic landscapes of rolling prairies, rugged canyons, and meandering rivers. The valley is also home to a variety of plant and animal species, including deer, coyotes, and migratory birds, making it a popular destination for nature enthusiasts and outdoor adventurers.

Whether you're exploring ancient petroglyphs, visiting historic landmarks, or simply enjoying the natural beauty of the valley, Picketwire Valley offers a journey through time and history that celebrates the rich cultural heritage and diverse landscapes of southeastern Colorado.

9. Bent's Old Fort National Historic Site

Bent's Old Fort National Historic Site, located near La Junta, Colorado, offers visitors a fascinating glimpse into the early days of the American West. Built in 1833 as a trading post along the Santa Fe Trail, Bent's Old Fort played a crucial role in the region's fur trade and served as a cultural crossroads where Native American tribes, traders, and pioneers converged.

One of the highlights of Bent's Old Fort is its meticulously reconstructed adobe fort, which faithfully recreates the original structure and provides visitors with an immersive experience of life on the frontier. Guided tours of the fort allow visitors to step back in time and explore its rooms, corridors, and courtyards, where costumed interpreters bring the history of the fort to life through demonstrations, reenactments, and interactive exhibits.

In addition to its fort, Bent's Old Fort National Historic Site offers a variety of programs and events that highlight the cultural and historical significance of the region. Visitors can attend living history demonstrations, special events, and educational programs that provide insight into the daily lives of the fort's inhabitants and the challenges they faced living on the frontier.

For those interested in the natural beauty of the area, Bent's Old Fort National Historic Site is surrounded by scenic landscapes of rolling prairies, rugged canyons, and meandering rivers, providing opportunities for hiking, wildlife viewing, and outdoor recreation. The site also features a visitor center with exhibits, artifacts, and information about the history and heritage of Bent's Old Fort and the Santa Fe Trail.

Whether you're exploring the fort's adobe walls, attending a living history demonstration, or simply enjoying the natural beauty of the surrounding landscape, Bent's Old Fort National Historic Site offers a fascinating and immersive experience that celebrates the rich cultural heritage and pioneering spirit of the American West.

10. La Junta

La Junta, nestled in the heart of southeastern Colorado, is a charming city steeped in history and culture. Named after the Spanish word for "the junction" due to its location where the Arkansas River and the Purgatoire River meet, La Junta has long been a crossroads of trade, travel, and cultural exchange.

One of the highlights of La Junta is its rich history as a key stop along the historic Santa Fe Trail. Visitors can explore the Santa Fe Trail Museum, which showcases artifacts, exhibits, and interactive displays that tell the story of the trail's role in shaping the history and culture of the American West. The museum also offers guided tours of Bent's Old Fort National Historic Site, a meticulously reconstructed adobe fort that served as a trading post along the Santa Fe Trail in the 19th century.

In addition to its historical attractions, La Junta offers a variety of cultural experiences for visitors to enjoy. The city is home to the Koshare Indian Museum, which houses one of the finest collections of Native American art and artifacts in the region, as well as the Koshare Indian Dancers, a renowned youth dance troupe that performs traditional Native American dances and ceremonies.

For outdoor enthusiasts, La Junta offers opportunities for hiking, birdwatching, and wildlife viewing amidst its scenic landscapes of rolling prairies, rugged canyons, and meandering rivers. The nearby Comanche National Grassland provides ample opportunities for outdoor recreation, with miles of trails, picnic areas, and campgrounds to explore.

Whether you're exploring the city's historical sites, experiencing its vibrant cultural scene, or enjoying the natural beauty of the surrounding landscape, La Junta offers a unique and memorable experience that celebrates the rich heritage and diverse landscapes of southeastern Colorado.

11. Withers Canyon/Dinosaur Footprints Trailhead

Withers Canyon, located near La Junta, Colorado, is a hidden gem for fossil enthusiasts and outdoor adventurers alike. This picturesque canyon is home to a fascinating array of dinosaur footprints, which offer a glimpse into the prehistoric past and provide opportunities for exploration and discovery.

One of the highlights of Withers Canyon is its Dinosaur Footprints Trailhead, which offers access to a network of hiking trails that wind through the canyon's scenic landscapes and lead to fossil-rich areas where visitors can view dinosaur footprints preserved in the rock. These footprints, made by ancient dinosaurs millions of years ago, offer valuable insight into the behavior, anatomy, and ecology of these long-extinct creatures.

In addition to its dinosaur footprints, Withers Canyon offers opportunities for hiking, birdwatching, and wildlife viewing amidst its rugged terrain and diverse ecosystems. The canyon is home to a variety of plant and animal species, including deer, coyotes, and migratory birds, making it a popular destination for nature enthusiasts and outdoor adventurers.

Whether you're exploring the canyon's fossil-rich landscapes, hiking its scenic trails, or simply enjoying the natural beauty of the surrounding area, Withers Canyon offers a unique and unforgettable experience that celebrates the wonders of the natural world and the mysteries of the prehistoric past.

12. Two Buttes Reservoir

Two Buttes Reservoir, located near Springfield, Colorado, is a tranquil oasis amidst the rolling plains of southeastern Colorado. This man-made reservoir, created by the construction of Two Buttes Dam in the early 20th century, offers visitors a scenic retreat where they can enjoy fishing, boating, and outdoor recreation amidst the beauty of the High Plains.

One of the highlights of Two Buttes Reservoir is its excellent fishing opportunities. Anglers can cast a line in search of catfish, walleye, bass, and other game fish that inhabit the reservoir's calm waters. The reservoir's remote location and peaceful surroundings make it a popular spot for fishing enthusiasts seeking a quiet and relaxing getaway.

In addition to its fishing opportunities, Two Buttes Reservoir offers a variety of recreational activities for visitors to enjoy. Boaters can explore the reservoir's waters by kayak, canoe, or motorboat, while hikers and birdwatchers can explore the surrounding area's scenic trails and diverse wildlife habitats. Picnic areas and campgrounds are also available for those looking to enjoy a leisurely day in the great outdoors.

Whether you're fishing on the reservoir, boating on the water, or simply enjoying the scenic beauty of the surrounding landscape, Two Buttes Reservoir offers a peaceful and rejuvenating retreat that celebrates the natural beauty and outdoor recreation opportunities of southeastern Colorado.

13. Comanche National Grassland

The Comanche National Grassland, located in southeastern Colorado near the towns of La Junta and Springfield, offers visitors a vast expanse of rolling prairies, rugged canyons, and scenic vistas to explore. With its diverse landscapes, rich history, and abundant wildlife, the grassland provides opportunities for outdoor recreation, cultural exploration, and scenic beauty amidst the beauty of the High Plains.

One of the highlights of the Comanche National Grassland is its rich cultural heritage and history. The grassland is home to a variety of archaeological sites and landmarks that offer insight into the lives and cultures of Native American tribes who have inhabited the area for thousands of years. Visitors can explore ancient ruins, rock art panels, and historic trails that tell the story of the region's indigenous peoples and their connection to the land.

In addition to its cultural heritage, the Comanche National Grassland offers opportunities for outdoor recreation and exploration. Visitors can hike, bike, or horseback ride along the grassland's scenic trails, which wind through diverse ecosystems such as grasslands, woodlands, and riparian areas. Birdwatchers and wildlife enthusiasts can spot a variety of bird species, including eagles, hawks, and migratory songbirds, as well as mammals such as deer, coyotes, and pronghorn antelope.

Whether you're exploring the grassland's cultural heritage, hiking its scenic trails, or simply enjoying the natural beauty of the surrounding landscape, the Comanche National Grassland offers a unique and unforgettable experience that celebrates the beauty, diversity, and heritage of southeastern Colorado.

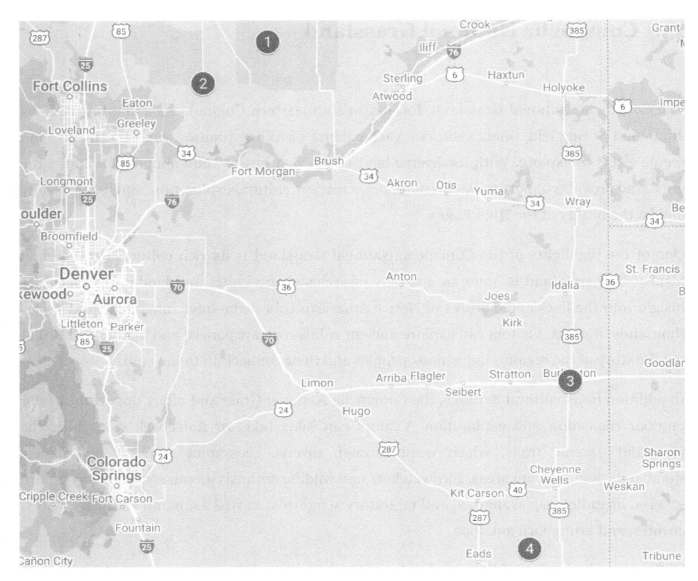

Eastern Plains Map 1 – Destinations 1-4

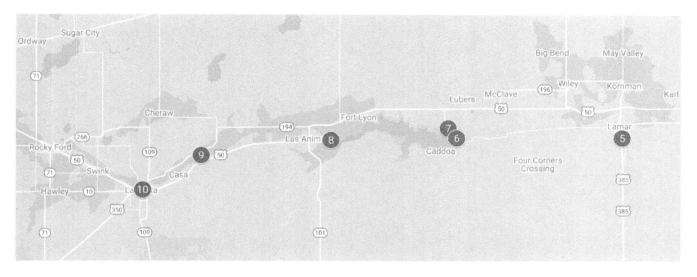

Eastern Plains Map 2 – Destinations 5-10

Eastern Plains Map 3 – Destinations 11-13

Rocky Mountains

1. Estes Park

Nestled in the heart of the Colorado Rockies, Estes Park is a charming mountain town that serves as the gateway to one of the most iconic national parks in the United States: Rocky Mountain National Park. Renowned for its breathtaking scenery, outdoor recreation opportunities, and vibrant arts and culture scene, Estes Park is a popular destination for nature lovers, adventure seekers, and families alike.

One of the highlights of Estes Park is its stunning natural beauty, with towering peaks, pristine lakes, and lush forests that provide a picturesque backdrop for outdoor adventures. Visitors can explore the miles of hiking trails that wind through Rocky Mountain National Park, offering opportunities to spot wildlife such as elk, mule deer, and bighorn sheep, as well as breathtaking vistas of snow-capped mountains and alpine meadows.

In addition to its outdoor recreation opportunities, Estes Park offers a variety of cultural attractions and activities for visitors to enjoy. The town is home to a vibrant arts community, with galleries, studios, and shops showcasing the work of local artists and artisans. Visitors can also explore historic landmarks such as the Stanley Hotel, which inspired Stephen King's novel "The Shining," or take a stroll along the scenic Riverwalk in downtown Estes Park.

For families with children, Estes Park offers a wide range of family-friendly activities and attractions, including amusement parks, miniature golf courses, and horseback riding tours. The town also hosts festivals, events, and concerts throughout the year, providing entertainment and excitement for visitors of all ages.

Whether you're hiking in the mountains, exploring the town's cultural attractions, or simply taking in the natural beauty of the surrounding landscape, Estes Park offers an unforgettable mountain getaway that celebrates the beauty, adventure, and spirit of the Colorado Rockies.

2. Moraine Park

Moraine Park, located in Rocky Mountain National Park near Estes Park, Colorado, is a serene and picturesque valley that offers visitors a tranquil escape into nature amidst the stunning beauty of the Colorado Rockies. Renowned for its lush meadows, scenic vistas, and abundant wildlife, Moraine Park is a popular destination for hiking, wildlife viewing, and outdoor recreation.

One of the highlights of Moraine Park is its stunning natural beauty, with expansive meadows surrounded by towering peaks that provide a picturesque backdrop for outdoor adventures. Visitors can explore the valley's network of hiking trails, which wind through grassy meadows, dense forests, and along meandering streams, offering opportunities to spot wildlife such as elk, deer, and moose, as well as breathtaking views of the surrounding mountains.

In addition to its hiking trails, Moraine Park offers a variety of recreational opportunities for visitors to enjoy. Anglers can cast a line in the Big Thompson River, which flows through the valley, in search of trout and other game fish, while birdwatchers can spot a variety of bird species, including eagles, hawks, and songbirds, as they soar overhead.

For those seeking a more leisurely experience, Moraine Park is an ideal spot for picnicking, wildlife watching, and photography, with its scenic vistas and abundant wildlife providing ample opportunities for relaxation and enjoyment. The valley is also home to several campgrounds, where visitors can spend the night under the stars and enjoy the tranquility of the natural surroundings.

3. Cub Lake

Cub Lake, located in Rocky Mountain National Park near Estes Park, Colorado, is a serene alpine lake that offers visitors a peaceful retreat into nature amidst the breathtaking beauty of the Colorado Rockies. Surrounded by towering peaks, dense forests, and lush meadows, Cub Lake is a popular destination for hiking, wildlife viewing, and photography.

One of the highlights of Cub Lake is its tranquil setting, with crystal-clear waters reflecting the surrounding mountains and forests, creating a picturesque backdrop for outdoor adventures. Visitors can hike to the lake along the Cub Lake Trail, which winds through dense forests and along meandering streams, offering opportunities to spot wildlife such as elk, deer, and moose, as well as breathtaking views of the surrounding landscape.

In addition to its natural beauty, Cub Lake offers a variety of recreational opportunities for visitors to enjoy. Anglers can cast a line in the lake's pristine waters, in search of trout and other game fish, while birdwatchers can spot a variety of bird species, including waterfowl, shorebirds, and songbirds, as they explore the shoreline.

For those seeking a more leisurely experience, Cub Lake is an ideal spot for picnicking, wildlife watching, and photography, with its scenic vistas and abundant wildlife providing ample opportunities for relaxation and enjoyment. The lake is also a popular destination for photographers, who come to capture the beauty of the surrounding landscape and the reflections of the mountains in the calm waters of the lake.

4. Rocky Mountain National Park

Rocky Mountain National Park, located in northern Colorado near the town of Estes Park, is a natural wonderland that attracts millions of visitors each year with its breathtaking scenery, diverse ecosystems, and abundance of outdoor recreational opportunities. Encompassing over 415 square miles of pristine wilderness, the park is a sanctuary for wildlife, a playground for outdoor enthusiasts, and a haven for nature lovers seeking to explore the beauty of the Colorado Rockies.

One of the highlights of Rocky Mountain National Park is its stunning alpine landscapes, which feature towering peaks, glacier-carved valleys, and lush meadows dotted with wildflowers. Visitors can explore the park's extensive network of hiking trails, which range from easy walks to challenging climbs, offering opportunities to experience the park's diverse ecosystems and spot wildlife such as elk, deer, and bighorn sheep.

In addition to its hiking trails, Rocky Mountain National Park offers a variety of recreational activities for visitors to enjoy. Anglers can cast a line in the park's pristine lakes and streams, in search of trout and other game fish, while birdwatchers can spot a variety of bird species, including eagles, hawks, and migratory songbirds, as they soar overhead.

For those seeking a more leisurely experience, Rocky Mountain National Park is an ideal spot for scenic drives, picnicking, and wildlife watching. The park is home to several scenic drives, including the Trail Ridge Road, which traverses the Continental Divide and offers breathtaking views of the surrounding mountains and valleys.

5.   Sprague Lake

Sprague Lake, located in Rocky Mountain National Park near Estes Park, Colorado, is a serene alpine lake that offers visitors a peaceful retreat amidst the stunning beauty of the Colorado Rockies. Surrounded by towering peaks, dense forests, and lush meadows, Sprague Lake is a popular destination for hiking, wildlife viewing, and photography.

One of the highlights of Sprague Lake is its tranquil setting, with crystal-clear waters reflecting the surrounding mountains and forests, creating a picturesque backdrop for outdoor adventures. Visitors can hike to the lake along the Sprague Lake Trail, a scenic loop trail that winds through dense forests and along the shores of the lake, offering opportunities to spot wildlife such as elk, deer, and moose, as well as breathtaking views of the surrounding landscape.

In addition to its natural beauty, Sprague Lake offers a variety of recreational opportunities for visitors to enjoy. Anglers can cast a line in the lake's pristine waters, in search of trout and other game fish, while birdwatchers can spot a variety of bird species, including waterfowl, shorebirds, and songbirds, as they explore the shoreline.

For those seeking a more leisurely experience, Sprague Lake is an ideal spot for picnicking, wildlife watching, and photography, with its scenic vistas and abundant wildlife providing ample opportunities for relaxation and enjoyment. The lake is also a popular destination for photographers, who come to capture the beauty of the surrounding landscape and the reflections of the mountains in the calm waters of the lake.

6. Lily Lake

Lily Lake, situated in Rocky Mountain National Park near Estes Park, Colorado, is a hidden gem that offers visitors a serene escape into nature amidst the breathtaking beauty of the Colorado Rockies. Surrounded by towering peaks, lush forests, and alpine meadows, Lily Lake is a popular destination for hiking, wildlife viewing, and photography.

One of the highlights of Lily Lake is its tranquil setting, with crystal-clear waters reflecting the surrounding mountains and forests, creating a picturesque backdrop for outdoor adventures. Visitors can hike to the lake along the Lily Lake Trail, a scenic loop trail that winds through dense forests and along the shores of the lake, offering opportunities to spot wildlife such as elk, deer, and moose, as well as breathtaking views of the surrounding landscape.

In addition to its natural beauty, Lily Lake offers a variety of recreational opportunities for visitors to enjoy. Anglers can cast a line in the lake's pristine waters, in search of trout and other game fish, while birdwatchers can spot a variety of bird species, including waterfowl, shorebirds, and songbirds, as they explore the shoreline.

For those seeking a more leisurely experience, Lily Lake is an ideal spot for picnicking, wildlife watching, and photography, with its scenic vistas and abundant wildlife providing ample opportunities for relaxation and enjoyment. The lake is also a popular destination for photographers, who come to capture the beauty of the surrounding landscape and the reflections of the mountains in the calm waters of the lake.

7.   Twin Sisters Peaks

Twin Sisters Peaks, standing proudly in Rocky Mountain National Park near Estes Park, Colorado, are a majestic pair of mountains that offer adventurous hikers stunning panoramic views and a sense of accomplishment. These iconic peaks, named for their resemblance to twin siblings when viewed from a distance, are a popular destination for outdoor enthusiasts seeking breathtaking vistas and a challenging ascent.

One of the highlights of Twin Sisters Peaks is the rewarding hike to their summit. The trail begins at the Twin Sisters Trailhead and winds its way through dense forests, across alpine meadows, and along rocky ridges, offering hikers a variety of terrain and scenery to enjoy along the way. As hikers ascend, they are treated to sweeping views of the surrounding mountains, valleys, and forests, providing a sense of awe and wonder at the natural beauty of the Colorado Rockies.

In addition to its stunning views, Twin Sisters Peaks offer hikers the opportunity to experience the thrill of summiting a challenging peak. The final push to the summit involves scrambling over rocky terrain and navigating narrow ridgelines, but the effort is rewarded with unparalleled views of the surrounding landscape stretching out in all directions.

For those seeking a less strenuous experience, the trail to Twin Sisters Peaks also offers opportunities for wildlife viewing, wildflower spotting, and photography. Visitors may encounter a variety of wildlife along the trail, including elk, deer, and marmots, as well as a colorful array of wildflowers that bloom in the alpine meadows during the summer months.

8. Alberta Falls

Alberta Falls, located in Rocky Mountain National Park near Estes Park, Colorado, is a stunning waterfall that offers visitors a glimpse into the beauty and power of nature. Fed by the glacial waters of Glacier Creek, Alberta Falls cascades over granite cliffs, creating a spectacle of rushing water and mist that delights visitors of all ages.

One of the highlights of Alberta Falls is its accessibility. The falls are easily reached via a short, family-friendly hike along the Alberta Falls Trail, which begins at the Glacier Gorge Trailhead and winds its way through dense forests and along the banks of Glacier Creek to the base of the falls. Along the way, hikers are treated to scenic views of the surrounding mountains, valleys, and forests, making it a popular destination for visitors looking for a quick and easy outdoor adventure.

In addition to its accessibility, Alberta Falls offers visitors the opportunity to experience the beauty and power of a mountain waterfall up close. The falls plunge over a series of granite cliffs, creating a mesmerizing display of cascading water and mist that captivates the senses and provides a refreshing respite from the summer heat.

For those seeking a longer and more challenging hike, the Alberta Falls Trail also serves as the starting point for a variety of other trails that lead deeper into Rocky Mountain National Park, offering opportunities for further exploration and adventure.

9. Glacier Gorge

Glacier Gorge, located in Rocky Mountain National Park near Estes Park, Colorado, is a spectacular alpine wonderland that offers visitors a glimpse into the breathtaking beauty and rugged grandeur of the Colorado Rockies. Surrounded by towering peaks, glacier-carved valleys, and pristine alpine lakes, Glacier Gorge is a popular destination for hikers, climbers, and outdoor enthusiasts seeking adventure and exploration amidst some of the park's most iconic landscapes.

One of the highlights of Glacier Gorge is its stunning scenery, with dramatic cliffs, cascading waterfalls, and lush forests that provide a picturesque backdrop for outdoor adventures. Visitors can explore the gorge's network of hiking trails, which wind through dense forests, along rushing streams, and past scenic viewpoints, offering opportunities to spot wildlife such as elk, deer, and bighorn sheep, as well as breathtaking vistas of the surrounding mountains and valleys.

In addition to its hiking trails, Glacier Gorge offers a variety of recreational opportunities for visitors to enjoy. Anglers can cast a line in the park's pristine lakes and streams, in search of trout and other game fish, while climbers can test their skills on the park's challenging rock faces and alpine routes. The gorge is also home to several scenic picnic areas and campgrounds, where visitors can relax and enjoy the natural beauty of the surrounding landscape.

10. Bear Lake

Bear Lake, nestled in the heart of Rocky Mountain National Park near Estes Park, Colorado, is a serene alpine lake that captivates visitors with its crystal-clear waters, stunning mountain views, and tranquil surroundings. Surrounded by towering peaks, dense forests, and lush meadows, Bear Lake is a popular destination for outdoor enthusiasts seeking to explore the beauty of the Colorado Rockies.

One of the highlights of Bear Lake is its accessibility. The lake is easily reached via a short, family-friendly hike along the Bear Lake Loop Trail, which circles the lake and offers opportunities for visitors of all ages and abilities to enjoy its scenic beauty. Along the way, hikers are treated to panoramic views of the surrounding mountains, valleys, and forests, making it a popular spot for picnicking, photography, and wildlife viewing.

In addition to its natural beauty, Bear Lake offers visitors the opportunity to explore the surrounding area's network of hiking trails, which wind through dense forests, along rushing streams, and past scenic viewpoints. The lake is also a popular destination for fishing, with its pristine waters teeming with trout and other game fish that attract anglers from near and far.

For those seeking a more leisurely experience, Bear Lake is an ideal spot for picnicking, wildlife watching, and relaxation, with its scenic vistas and tranquil surroundings providing the perfect backdrop for a day of outdoor enjoyment. Visitors can also explore the nearby Bear Lake Nature Trail, which offers interpretive signs and exhibits that provide insight into the natural history and ecology of the area.

Whether you're hiking around the lake, picnicking by the shore, or simply taking in the natural beauty of the surrounding landscape, Bear Lake offers a serene and rejuvenating escape into nature that celebrates the beauty, diversity, and spirit of Rocky Mountain National Park.

11. Emerald Lake

Emerald Lake, situated in Rocky Mountain National Park near Estes Park, Colorado, is a breathtaking alpine lake that dazzles visitors with its stunning turquoise waters, towering peaks, and pristine wilderness surroundings. Named for the vibrant hue of its waters, which are fed by melting snow and glaciers, Emerald Lake is a popular destination for hikers, photographers, and nature lovers seeking to experience the beauty of the Colorado Rockies.

One of the highlights of Emerald Lake is its scenic beauty, with dramatic cliffs, cascading waterfalls, and lush forests that provide a picturesque backdrop for outdoor adventures. The lake is easily reached via a moderate hike along the Emerald Lake Trail, which winds its way through dense forests, across alpine meadows, and along rushing streams, offering opportunities to spot wildlife such as elk, deer, and bighorn sheep, as well as breathtaking vistas of the surrounding mountains and valleys.

In addition to its stunning scenery, Emerald Lake offers visitors the opportunity to experience the thrill of summiting a challenging peak. The final push to the lake involves scrambling over rocky terrain and navigating narrow ridgelines, but the effort is rewarded with unparalleled views of the surrounding landscape stretching out in all directions.

For those seeking a more leisurely experience, Emerald Lake is an ideal spot for picnicking, wildlife watching, and relaxation, with its scenic vistas and tranquil surroundings providing the perfect backdrop for a day of outdoor enjoyment. Visitors can also explore the nearby trails, which offer opportunities for further exploration and adventure.

12.   Grand Lake

Grand Lake, situated on the western edge of Rocky Mountain National Park in Colorado, is a charming mountain town and recreational paradise that offers visitors a gateway to adventure amidst the stunning beauty of the Colorado Rockies. Surrounded by towering peaks, dense forests, and pristine alpine lakes, Grand Lake is a popular destination for outdoor enthusiasts seeking to explore the natural wonders of the Rocky Mountains.

One of the highlights of Grand Lake is its namesake lake, which is the largest natural lake in Colorado and offers a variety of recreational opportunities for visitors to enjoy. Anglers can cast a line in the lake's crystal-clear waters, in search of trout, salmon, and other game fish, while boaters can explore its scenic shoreline and secluded coves by kayak, canoe, or motorboat.

In addition to its outdoor recreational opportunities, Grand Lake offers a variety of cultural attractions and activities for visitors to enjoy. The town is home to a vibrant arts community, with galleries, studios, and shops showcasing the work of local artists and artisans. Visitors can also explore historic landmarks such as the Grand Lake Lodge, which offers panoramic views of the surrounding mountains and valleys, or take a stroll along the scenic boardwalk that winds along the shores of the lake.

For those seeking a more leisurely experience, Grand Lake is an ideal spot for picnicking, wildlife watching, and relaxation, with its scenic vistas and tranquil surroundings providing the perfect backdrop for a day of outdoor enjoyment. The town is also home to several restaurants, cafes, and shops where visitors can sample local cuisine, browse for souvenirs, or simply soak in the laid-back mountain vibe.

Whether you're exploring the lake, hiking in the mountains, or simply taking in the natural beauty of the surrounding landscape, Grand Lake offers an unforgettable experience that celebrates the beauty, diversity, and spirit of the Colorado Rockies.

13. Trail Ridge Road

Trail Ridge Road, often referred to as the "highway to the sky," is a spectacular scenic drive that winds its way through Rocky Mountain National Park in Colorado. Stretching for 48 miles, this iconic roadway is renowned for its breathtaking views, high elevation, and rugged alpine landscapes, making it one of the most scenic drives in the United States.

One of the highlights of Trail Ridge Road is its dramatic elevation gain, reaching a peak elevation of over 12,000 feet at its highest point. As drivers ascend into the alpine tundra, they are treated to sweeping panoramic views of the surrounding mountains, valleys, and forests, with opportunities to spot wildlife such as elk, deer, and bighorn sheep along the way.

In addition to its stunning scenery, Trail Ridge Road offers visitors the opportunity to experience the unique ecosystems of Rocky Mountain National Park up close. The road passes through a variety of habitats, from dense forests and alpine meadows to rocky tundra and snow-capped peaks, providing a glimpse into the diverse flora and fauna that call the park home.

For those seeking outdoor adventure, Trail Ridge Road serves as a gateway to a variety of recreational opportunities, including hiking, wildlife viewing, and photography. Visitors can explore the park's network of hiking trails, which range from easy walks to challenging climbs, offering opportunities to experience the beauty and solitude of the Colorado Rockies.

14. Nederland

Nederland, nestled in the foothills of the Colorado Rockies, is a quirky mountain town with a unique charm and laid-back vibe. Known for its colorful storefronts, eclectic shops, and vibrant arts scene, Nederland is a popular destination for visitors seeking a taste of mountain culture and outdoor adventure.

One of the highlights of Nederland is its vibrant arts and music scene, with galleries, studios, and live music venues showcasing the work of local artists and musicians. Visitors can explore the town's historic downtown area, which is home to a variety of shops, boutiques, and cafes offering everything from handmade crafts to locally brewed beer.

In addition to its arts and culture scene, Nederland offers a variety of outdoor recreational opportunities for visitors to enjoy. The town is surrounded by scenic forests, alpine meadows, and rugged mountain peaks, providing ample opportunities for hiking, mountain biking, and wildlife viewing.

For those seeking a more leisurely experience, Nederland is an ideal spot for picnicking, exploring scenic drives, and soaking in the natural beauty of the surrounding landscape. The town is also home to several parks and open spaces, where visitors can relax and enjoy the mountain scenery.

15. Winter Park

Winter Park, nestled in the heart of the Colorado Rockies, is a premier destination for outdoor enthusiasts seeking adventure and excitement amidst the stunning beauty of the mountains. Known for its world-class skiing and snowboarding, as well as its scenic hiking and mountain biking trails, Winter Park offers something for visitors of all ages and interests.

One of the highlights of Winter Park is its renowned ski resort, which boasts over 3,000 acres of skiable terrain, including groomed runs, moguls, and terrain parks for all skill levels. With an average of over 300 inches of snowfall each year, the resort offers excellent conditions for winter sports enthusiasts seeking thrills and excitement on the slopes.

In addition to its skiing and snowboarding, Winter Park offers a variety of other outdoor recreational opportunities for visitors to enjoy. The town is surrounded by scenic forests, alpine meadows, and rugged mountain peaks, providing ample opportunities for hiking, mountain biking, and wildlife viewing.

For those seeking a more leisurely experience, Winter Park is an ideal spot for picnicking, fishing, and exploring scenic drives, with several parks, lakes, and open spaces to enjoy. The town also hosts a variety of events and festivals throughout the year, celebrating the culture, heritage, and natural beauty of the Colorado Rockies.

16. Idaho Springs

Idaho Springs, nestled in the foothills of the Rocky Mountains in Colorado, is a charming and historic town known for its rich mining heritage, outdoor recreation opportunities, and scenic beauty. Founded during the Colorado Gold Rush of the 19th century, Idaho Springs retains much of its historic character, with Victorian-era buildings, quaint shops, and cozy cafes lining its charming downtown streets.

One of the highlights of Idaho Springs is its fascinating mining history, which is showcased at the Argo Mill and Tunnel, a historic gold mine that offers guided tours and gold panning experiences for visitors. The town is also home to the Idaho Springs Heritage Museum, which provides insight into the area's mining heritage and cultural history through exhibits, artifacts, and interactive displays.

In addition to its historic attractions, Idaho Springs offers a variety of outdoor recreational opportunities for visitors to enjoy. The town is surrounded by scenic mountains, rushing rivers, and pristine forests, providing ample opportunities for hiking, fishing, mountain biking, and wildlife viewing. Nearby attractions include the Mount Evans Scenic Byway, which offers breathtaking views of the surrounding mountains and valleys, as well as the Indian Hot Springs, a natural hot spring resort that provides relaxation and rejuvenation for visitors.

For those seeking a more leisurely experience, Idaho Springs is an ideal spot for shopping, dining, and exploring the town's charming streets and historic landmarks. Visitors can browse for souvenirs at the town's eclectic shops and galleries, sample locally brewed beer at one of its breweries, or enjoy a delicious meal at a cozy restaurant.

17. Mount Evans Scenic Byway

The Mount Evans Scenic Byway, located in the Rocky Mountains of Colorado, is one of the highest paved roads in North America, offering visitors a breathtaking journey to the summit of Mount Evans, one of the state's iconic Fourteeners. Stretching for 28 miles from Idaho Springs to the summit of Mount Evans, the byway winds its way through rugged alpine landscapes, offering stunning views of snow-capped peaks, deep valleys, and pristine mountain lakes along the way.

One of the highlights of the Mount Evans Scenic Byway is its dramatic elevation gain, reaching a peak elevation of over 14,000 feet at the summit of Mount Evans. As drivers ascend into the alpine tundra, they are treated to sweeping panoramic views of the surrounding mountains, valleys, and forests, with opportunities to spot wildlife such as bighorn sheep, mountain goats, and marmots along the way.

In addition to its stunning scenery, the Mount Evans Scenic Byway offers visitors the opportunity to experience the unique ecosystems of the Rocky Mountains up close. The road passes through a variety of habitats, from dense forests and alpine meadows to rocky tundra and snow-capped peaks, providing a glimpse into the diverse flora and fauna that call the area home.

For those seeking outdoor adventure, the Mount Evans Scenic Byway serves as a gateway to a variety of recreational opportunities, including hiking, wildlife viewing, and photography. Visitors can explore the park's network of hiking trails, which range from easy walks to challenging climbs, offering opportunities to experience the beauty and solitude of the Colorado Rockies.

18. Mount Blue Sky Scenic Drive

Mount Blue Sky Scenic Drive, located in the heart of the Rocky Mountains in Colorado, is a stunning scenic drive that offers visitors a journey through alpine splendor amidst some of the most breathtaking landscapes in the state. Stretching for 45 miles from Idaho Springs to the summit of Mount Blue Sky, the scenic drive winds its way through rugged mountain terrain, offering panoramic views of snow-capped peaks, deep valleys, and pristine alpine lakes along the way.

One of the highlights of the Mount Blue Sky Scenic Drive is its dramatic elevation gain, reaching a peak elevation of over 13,000 feet at the summit of Mount Blue Sky. As drivers ascend into the alpine tundra, they are treated to sweeping vistas of the surrounding mountains, valleys, and forests, with opportunities to spot wildlife such as elk, deer, and bighorn sheep along the way.

In addition to its stunning scenery, the Mount Blue Sky Scenic Drive offers visitors the opportunity to experience the unique ecosystems of the Rocky Mountains up close. The road passes through a variety of habitats, from dense forests and alpine meadows to rocky tundra and snow-capped peaks, providing a glimpse into the diverse flora and fauna that call the area home.

For those seeking outdoor adventure, the Mount Blue Sky Scenic Drive serves as a gateway to a variety of recreational opportunities, including hiking, mountain biking, and wildlife viewing. Visitors can explore the park's network of trails, which range from easy walks to challenging climbs, offering opportunities to experience the beauty and solitude of the Colorado Rockies.

Whether you're driving along the scenic drive, stopping at overlooks to take in the views, or exploring the park's trails and wildlife habitats, Mount Blue Sky Scenic Drive offers an unforgettable journey through some of the most breathtaking landscapes in the Rocky Mountains.

19. Georgetown Loop Railroad

The Georgetown Loop Railroad, located in Georgetown, Colorado, is a historic narrow-gauge railroad that offers visitors a journey back in time to the heyday of Colorado's mining industry. Built in the late 19th century to transport silver ore from the mines to the mills, the railroad is now a popular tourist attraction that provides a scenic and nostalgic experience for visitors of all ages.

One of the highlights of the Georgetown Loop Railroad is its stunning route, which winds its way through rugged mountain terrain, across towering trestles, and alongside rushing streams. The railroad's historic steam locomotives and vintage passenger cars add to the charm of the journey, transporting passengers back to the era of the Wild West and the Colorado Gold Rush.

In addition to its scenic beauty, the Georgetown Loop Railroad offers visitors the opportunity to learn about the area's rich mining history through interpretive exhibits, guided tours, and demonstrations of historic mining equipment. The railroad also offers special events throughout the year, including holiday-themed train rides, dinner trains, and photography excursions.

For those seeking outdoor adventure, Georgetown is an ideal spot for hiking, mountain biking, and exploring scenic drives. The town is surrounded by rugged peaks, dense forests, and rushing rivers, providing ample opportunities for outdoor recreation and exploration.

20. Breckenridge

Breckenridge, nestled in the heart of the Colorado Rockies, is a charming mountain town known for its historic charm, vibrant culture, and world-class outdoor recreation opportunities. Founded during the Colorado Gold Rush of the 19th century, Breckenridge retains much of its historic character, with Victorian-era buildings, quaint shops, and lively restaurants lining its picturesque streets.

One of the highlights of Breckenridge is its world-class ski resort, which boasts over 2,900 acres of skiable terrain, including groomed runs, terrain parks, and backcountry skiing opportunities. With an average of over 300 inches of snowfall each year, the resort offers excellent conditions for skiers and snowboarders of all skill levels, making it a popular destination for winter sports enthusiasts from around the world.

In addition to its skiing and snowboarding, Breckenridge offers a variety of other outdoor recreational opportunities for visitors to enjoy. The town is surrounded by scenic mountains, rushing rivers, and pristine forests, providing ample opportunities for hiking, mountain biking, fishing, and wildlife viewing.

For those seeking a more leisurely experience, Breckenridge is an ideal spot for shopping, dining, and exploring its historic landmarks. Visitors can browse for souvenirs at the town's eclectic shops and galleries, sample locally brewed beer at one of its breweries, or enjoy a delicious meal at a cozy restaurant.

Whether you're hitting the slopes for a day of skiing, exploring the town's shops and galleries, or simply taking in the natural beauty of the surrounding landscape, Breckenridge offers an unforgettable experience that celebrates the beauty, culture, and spirit of the Colorado Rockies.

21. Vail

Vail, located in the heart of the Colorado Rockies, is a world-class destination for outdoor enthusiasts seeking adventure, excitement, and relaxation amidst some of the most stunning landscapes in the United States. Known for its legendary skiing and snowboarding, as well as its scenic hiking trails, lively village atmosphere, and luxurious amenities, Vail offers something for visitors of all ages and interests.

One of the highlights of Vail is its renowned ski resort, which boasts over 5,000 acres of skiable terrain, including groomed runs, moguls, and terrain parks for all skill levels. With an average of over 300 inches of snowfall each year, the resort offers excellent conditions for winter sports enthusiasts seeking thrills and excitement on the slopes.

In addition to its skiing and snowboarding, Vail offers a variety of other outdoor recreational opportunities for visitors to enjoy. The town is surrounded by scenic mountains, rushing rivers, and pristine forests, providing ample opportunities for hiking, mountain biking, fishing, and wildlife viewing.

For those seeking a more leisurely experience, Vail is an ideal spot for shopping, dining, and exploring its charming village atmosphere. Visitors can browse for souvenirs at the town's upscale shops and boutiques, sample gourmet cuisine at one of its world-class restaurants, or enjoy a relaxing spa treatment at one of its luxury resorts.

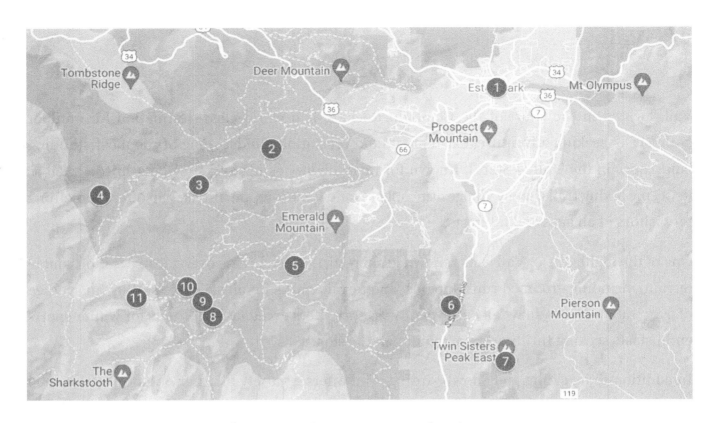

Rocky Mountains Map 1 – Destinations 1-11

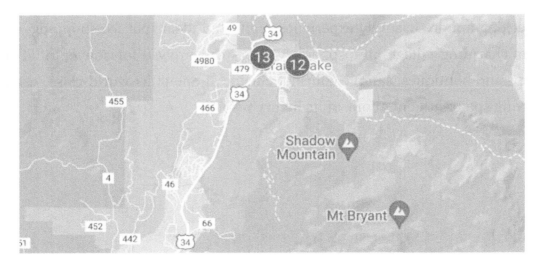

Rocky Mountains Map 2 – Destinations 12-13

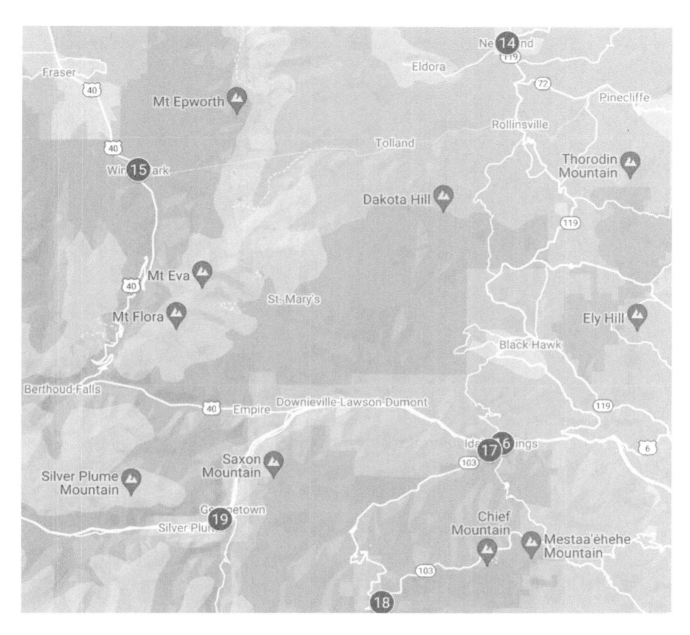

Rocky Mountains Map 3 – Destinations 14-19

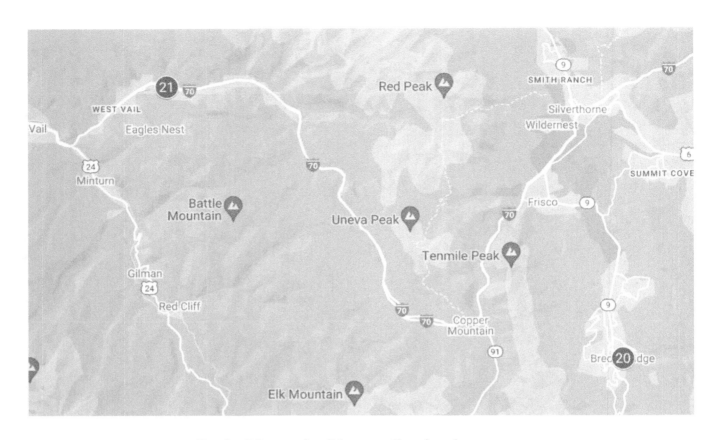

Rocky Mountains Map 4 – Destinations 20-21

Western Slope

1.   Hanging Lake

Hanging Lake is a stunning example of nature's artwork nestled in the heart of Colorado's Glenwood Canyon. This geological marvel is renowned for its strikingly clear, turquoise waters, which owe their unique coloration to dissolved carbonate minerals. The lake is delicately perched atop a cliff, and its edges are beautifully adorned with lush vegetation and delicate waterfalls, creating a serene and almost ethereal atmosphere.

The creation of Hanging Lake is a tale of geological transformation spanning thousands of years. It was formed by a geological fault, which caused the lake bed to drop away from the valley floor above. Over millennia, water flowing down from the cliffs above deposited dissolved limestone, which created the natural dam that holds the lake's waters today. This process, known as travertine deposition, continues to shape the lake's unique appearance.

Hanging Lake is not just a feast for the eyes but also a haven for diverse plant and animal life. The ecosystem around the lake is delicate, hosting species that have adapted to the unique environment of the high desert canyon. Visitors may spot various birds, small mammals, and a variety of aquatic life, making it a rewarding experience for nature enthusiasts.

The significance of Hanging Lake extends beyond its natural beauty. It is recognized as a National Natural Landmark, highlighting its importance in the natural heritage of the United States. This designation underlines the need for preservation and responsible visitation to ensure that future generations can continue to enjoy its beauty.

2.   Hanging Lake Trail

The Hanging Lake Trail offers one of the most iconic hiking experiences in Colorado. This steep, rugged path winds its way up through Glenwood Canyon, culminating at the breathtaking Hanging Lake. The trail covers approximately 1.2 miles (1.9 km) one way, with an elevation gain of over 1,000 feet (305 meters), making it a challenging yet rewarding endeavor.

As hikers ascend the trail, they are treated to a variety of scenic vistas and natural wonders. The path crosses crystal-clear streams, wanders through lush forests, and offers spectacular views of the canyon's rugged cliffs. Along the way, informational signs provide insights into the area's geological history and the unique ecosystem supported by this environment.

One of the most remarkable features encountered on the Hanging Lake Trail is Spouting Rock. This natural wonder, a waterfall that flows through a hole in the limestone cliff face, offers a cool respite and a spectacular photo opportunity for hikers.

Given the trail's popularity and the delicate nature of Hanging Lake's ecosystem, visitors are encouraged to practice Leave No Trace principles. This includes staying on designated trails, packing out all trash, and respecting wildlife and plant life. In recent years, a permit system has been implemented to manage visitor numbers and minimize environmental impact.

3.   Glenwood Springs

The hot springs in Glenwood Springs are among its most famous attractions, drawing visitors from around the world. The largest of these, the Glenwood Hot Springs Pool, is considered one of the largest mineral hot springs pools in the world. These therapeutic waters have been a gathering place for centuries, first for Indigenous peoples and later for settlers drawn by the promise of health benefits.

Beyond its hot springs, Glenwood Springs serves as a gateway to a plethora of outdoor activities. The surrounding mountains and rivers provide ample opportunities for hiking, biking, skiing, and whitewater rafting. The town is also a stone's throw away from the majestic Hanging Lake and the challenging Hanging Lake Trail, making it a hub for nature enthusiasts and adventure seekers alike.

Glenwood Springs is not only about natural beauty and outdoor pursuits; it's steeped in history as well. The town's historical architecture, museums, and the famous Hotel Colorado tell the story of the area's development from a mining town to a premier resort destination. The town also boasts connections to famous figures, including Doc Holliday, whose final resting place is rumored to be in the local cemetery.

Whether it's soaking in the healing mineral waters, exploring the natural beauty of the Colorado landscape, or delving into the rich tapestry of history, Glenwood Springs offers a diverse array of experiences that cater to all who visit.

4.   Rifle Falls State Park

Rifle Falls State Park, nestled in the heart of Colorado, is a breathtaking natural sanctuary known for its signature triple waterfall, cascading 70 feet into a lush valley. This stunning spectacle is not only a visual marvel but also supports a unique microclimate around the falls, fostering a variety of plant life unusual for the region. The park's beauty extends beyond the waterfalls to include intriguing limestone caves and small caverns formed by natural erosion, offering visitors a chance to explore and discover the hidden wonders within.

With a network of hiking trails ranging from easy walks to more challenging treks, the park caters to all levels of outdoor enthusiasts. Trails like the Coyote Trail loop around the falls, provide access to the caves, and reveal the area's diverse flora and fauna, making it a haven for nature lovers and wildlife watchers alike. Mule deer, elk, and numerous bird species, including red-tailed hawks and golden eagles, are commonly spotted, enriching the visitor experience with opportunities for bird watching and wildlife photography.

Rifle Falls State Park also offers camping facilities close to the waterfall, allowing guests to immerse themselves in nature's tranquility overnight. The sound of the cascading water creates a serene backdrop for campers, while picnic areas offer spots for peaceful lunches amidst nature. The campground is equipped with amenities that ensure a comfortable stay for those wishing to extend their visit and absorb the park's natural beauty at a slower pace.

The park is a year-round destination, with each season offering a unique perspective on its natural beauty. Spring and summer highlight the vigor of the falls and the bloom of wildflowers, while autumn transforms the landscape with a palette of warm colors. Winter occasionally freezes the falls, creating spectacular ice formations that add to the park's magical appeal.

Conservation efforts are vital to preserving the delicate ecosystems of Rifle Falls State Park. Visitors are encouraged to follow Leave No Trace principles to minimize their impact on the environment, ensuring the park remains a pristine and inspiring natural retreat for future generations. Whether seeking adventure, relaxation, or a deeper connection with nature, Rifle Falls State Park stands as a testament to Colorado's extraordinary natural diversity, offering an unforgettable experience to all who visit.

5. Colorado National Monument

Colorado National Monument is a stunning showcase of the natural beauty and grandeur of the American West, located near Grand Junction on the Colorado Plateau. This breathtaking park spans over 20,000 acres and features a dramatic landscape of towering monoliths, vast plateaus, and deep canyons, all carved from the vibrant red sandstone that defines the region. The monument is a testament to millions of years of erosion and geological activity, offering visitors a glimpse into the Earth's dynamic history.

The monument's most iconic features include towering rock formations such as Independence Monument, the Kissing Couple, and the Coke Ovens, whose names reflect their unique shapes and the imaginative spirit they inspire in visitors. These formations stand as silent sentinels over the landscape, bearing witness to the passage of time. The Rim Rock Drive, a 23-mile scenic road that winds through the heart of the park, offers panoramic views of these spectacular landscapes, making it a must-do for anyone visiting the area. Along the drive, numerous overlooks and trailheads provide opportunities to stop, explore, and soak in the monument's majestic beauty.

Hiking in Colorado National Monument is a rewarding experience, with over 40 miles of trails that range from easy strolls to challenging backcountry treks. Trails like the Serpents Trail, originally built as a road in the early 20th century, and the Monument Canyon Trail, which passes by the base of Independence Monument and other significant rock formations, offer immersive experiences of the park's unique geology and desert ecosystem. Hikers may encounter a variety of wildlife, including desert bighorn sheep, golden eagles, and a diverse array of plant species adapted to the harsh desert environment.

The monument is not just a haven for hikers and sightseers; it also plays a crucial role in conservation and education. It serves as an outdoor laboratory for scientists studying geology, ecology, and archaeology, while also offering educational programs and ranger-led activities that enlighten visitors about the area's natural history and the importance of preserving these landscapes for future generations.

6. Grand Junction

Grand Junction, nestled in the heart of Colorado's Western Slope, serves as a vibrant hub of outdoor adventure, cultural richness, and geological wonders. This city, the largest in the region, stands out for its unique location at the confluence of the Colorado and Gunnison rivers, making it a central point for exploring the natural beauty and recreational activities that Colorado is famous for. Grand Junction's landscape is a striking mix of desert vistas, lush vineyards, and the dramatic rock formations of the nearby Colorado National Monument, providing a diverse backdrop for all who visit.

The city is renowned for its thriving wine industry, with numerous vineyards and wineries dotting the surrounding area. The Grand Valley AVA (American Viticultural Area) is Colorado's wine country, where visitors can indulge in wine tastings and tours, experiencing firsthand the region's dedication to viticulture and enology. These wine tours not only offer a taste of some of the state's finest wines but also reveal the stunning scenery and agricultural landscape that define the valley.

Outdoor enthusiasts find Grand Junction an irresistible destination. The nearby Colorado National Monument offers miles of hiking and biking trails through red rock canyons and towering monoliths, while the Grand Mesa, the world's largest flat-topped mountain, provides opportunities for fishing, hiking, and skiing, depending on the season. The city itself is crisscrossed with bike paths and green spaces, encouraging an active and outdoor lifestyle.

Culturally, Grand Junction does not disappoint. Downtown, Main Street is lined with art galleries, shops, restaurants, and historic buildings, reflecting the community's commitment to preserving its heritage while embracing modernity. The city hosts a variety of events and festivals throughout the year, including the Colorado Mountain Winefest and the Grand Junction Off-Road, drawing visitors and locals alike to celebrate the unique spirit and beauty of the region.

Grand Junction's blend of natural beauty, recreational opportunities, and cultural vitality make it a standout destination in Colorado.

7. Grand Mesa Scenic Byway

The Grand Mesa Scenic Byway, also known as Colorado State Highway 65, is a journey through some of Colorado's most breathtaking landscapes, leading adventurers through the heart of the world's largest flat-topped mountain, the Grand Mesa. This scenic route stretches approximately 63 miles from the arid desert landscapes near Cedaredge, through lush alpine forests and meadows, to the vibrant city of Grand Junction, providing a stunning contrast of Colorado's diverse ecosystems.

As travelers ascend the byway from either end, they are greeted with dramatic changes in scenery. Starting from the lower elevations, the road meanders through orchards and vineyards, climbing into dense forests of aspen and spruce, and opening up to reveal expansive vistas of the Grand Mesa. This plateau rises over 11,000 feet above sea level and is dotted with more than 300 lakes, offering spectacular views that stretch to the horizon, where rugged mountain peaks meet the blue sky.

The Grand Mesa Scenic Byway is not just a road; it's an invitation to explore. Along the route, numerous pull-offs and viewpoints offer chances to pause and soak in the panoramic landscapes. Recreational opportunities abound, with access to hiking trails, fishing spots, and picnic areas, making it easy for travelers to connect with nature at their own pace. In the winter, the Grand Mesa transforms into a wonderland for snow sports, with cross-country skiing, snowshoeing, and snowmobiling taking center stage.

This scenic byway also serves as a gateway to understanding the area's rich history and geology. Informational signs along the route provide insights into the natural and human history of the region, from its geological formation to its use by Native American tribes and early settlers. The Land's End Observatory, near the byway's western end, offers not only sweeping views but also a glimpse into the past with its historic stone tower.

The Grand Mesa Scenic Byway is more than just a road; it's a journey through time and nature. It encapsulates the essence of Colorado's natural beauty, offering a diverse array of experiences that appeal to nature lovers, adventurers, and those seeking solace in the great outdoors.

8.   Paonia State Park

Paonia State Park, nestled in the picturesque valley of the North Fork Gunnison River in Western Colorado, is a captivating natural retreat known for its rugged beauty and tranquil atmosphere. This relatively small but immensely scenic park spans a diverse landscape that ranges from arid sagebrush hills to dense forests, with the sparkling waters of the Paonia Reservoir at its heart. The park offers a serene escape for those looking to immerse themselves in nature, away from the hustle and bustle of more crowded destinations.

One of the park's main attractions is the Paonia Reservoir, a haven for water enthusiasts. During the warmer months, the reservoir becomes a popular spot for boating, fishing, and paddleboarding. Anglers can enjoy casting their lines in the hopes of catching rainbow trout, yellow perch, and kokanee salmon, among other species. The surrounding areas also offer picturesque spots for picnicking and wildlife watching, where visitors might catch glimpses of deer, elk, and a variety of bird species that call this area home.

The beauty of Paonia State Park extends beyond its water activities. The park is cradled by steep mountain slopes and rugged cliffs, creating a dramatic backdrop for hiking and exploration. Although the park has limited developed trails, the surrounding Gunnison National Forest provides ample opportunities for hiking, with paths that meander through diverse ecosystems and offer breathtaking views of the valley below.

Photographers and nature lovers alike are drawn to Paonia State Park for its stunning natural vistas and the ever-changing light that dances across the landscape. The transition from day to night unveils a spectacular night sky, free from light pollution, making it an ideal spot for stargazing and experiencing the tranquil beauty of the cosmos.

Paonia State Park's charm lies in its simplicity and the unspoiled beauty of its natural environment. It serves as a reminder of the serene wilderness that can still be found within Colorado's borders. For those seeking solace in the great outdoors, a visit to Paonia State Park offers a chance to reconnect with nature, find peace by the water, and explore the rugged landscapes that make this area uniquely captivating.

9. Maroon Bells

Maroon Bells, located just outside of Aspen, Colorado, in the heart of the Rocky Mountains, are two of the most iconic and photographed peaks in all of North America. Maroon Peak and North Maroon Peak, standing at 14,163 feet and 14,019 feet respectively, are famed for their striking maroon hue and symmetrically mirrored reflection in the crystal-clear Maroon Lake. This breathtaking scene, framed by pristine forests and wildflower-dotted meadows, encapsulates the essence of Colorado's rugged beauty, drawing visitors from around the globe.

The journey to Maroon Bells is an experience in itself. Access is thoughtfully controlled to preserve the natural environment, with shuttle buses from Aspen Highlands offering a convenient way to reach the area during peak season. Once there, visitors are greeted by a landscape that feels almost otherworldly in its beauty. The peaks, part of the Elk Mountains, owe their distinctive maroon color to the weathering of hematite, an iron oxide, giving the mountains their name and unique appearance.

Maroon Lake, situated at the base of the peaks, provides one of the most captivating viewpoints. The lake's still waters offer a perfect mirror to the towering peaks above, creating a mesmerizing and highly photogenic scene, especially at sunrise and sunset when the light casts a golden glow over the landscape.

Hiking in the Maroon Bells-Snowmass Wilderness offers trails for every level of outdoor enthusiast, from leisurely walks around Maroon Lake to more challenging treks into the wilderness. The Maroon Bells Scenic Loop and the Crater Lake trail are popular choices, providing stunning views and encounters with the area's rich biodiversity. Adventurous hikers and mountaineers can tackle the more strenuous and technical climbs to the summits of the Maroon Bells, though these are known for their difficulty and require experience and preparation.

Beyond their physical allure, Maroon Bells are steeped in ecological significance. The area is a habitat for an abundance of wildlife, including elk, mule deer, and black bears, and is a vital part of the larger ecosystem of the White River National Forest.

10. Aspen

Nestled high in the Elk Mountains branch of the Rockies, is a blend of opulent resort living and rugged natural beauty, offering a unique fusion of luxury and wilderness that attracts visitors from around the world. Renowned for its world-class skiing, upscale shopping, fine dining, and vibrant cultural scene, Aspen embodies the pinnacle of outdoor recreation and cosmopolitan sophistication.

In winter, Aspen's four major ski areas – Aspen Mountain, Aspen Highlands, Buttermilk, and Snowmass – become the town's heartbeat, drawing ski enthusiasts of all skill levels to their meticulously groomed slopes and challenging backcountry terrain. Buttermilk is famed for its family-friendly atmosphere and terrain parks, while Aspen Mountain, right above the downtown area, caters to a more experienced crowd with its steep, expert runs. Snowmass, the largest of the four, offers a vast array of trails that cater to every level, alongside a bustling village scene. Aspen Highlands boasts the legendary Highland Bowl, offering some of the most exhilarating in-bounds backcountry skiing in North America.

Beyond the slopes, Aspen shines in all seasons. Summer and fall reveal a different side of the town's beauty, with wildflower-strewn trails, glistening alpine lakes, and vibrant autumn colors. Hiking, mountain biking, and fly fishing are popular activities, offering visitors the chance to immerse themselves in the stunning Rocky Mountain landscape. The Maroon Bells, just a short drive from Aspen, provide one of the most iconic backdrops for outdoor adventures in the United States.

Culturally, Aspen is unparalleled. Home to the Aspen Music Festival and School, the town thrives with classical music performances throughout the summer. Art enthusiasts will find a wealth of galleries and museums, and the annual Aspen Ideas Festival attracts thinkers and leaders from around the globe to discuss pressing global issues.

Despite its fame and affluence, Aspen remains deeply connected to its roots as a silver mining town. This history is reflected in its Victorian architecture and in the spirit of community that pervades. From its humble beginnings to its current status as a premier global destination, Aspen offers a unique mix of natural beauty, history, and luxury living.

11. Independence Pass

Independence Pass, towering at an elevation of 12,095 feet, is one of Colorado's most breathtaking and iconic mountain passes. It connects Aspen to the east with Twin Lakes to the west, traversing the Continental Divide through the Sawatch Range. This scenic route, part of Colorado State Highway 82, is a marvel of engineering, offering dramatic views, rugged terrain, and a sense of adventure that draws travelers, cyclists, and photographers from across the globe.

Open typically from Memorial Day through late October, weather permitting, the pass is a narrow, winding road that demands careful navigation but rewards travelers with unparalleled vistas of alpine landscapes, lush valleys, and snow-capped peaks. The journey along Independence Pass is as memorable as the destinations it connects, featuring steep ascents, sharp curves, and thrilling drop-offs, all while surrounded by the raw beauty of the Rocky Mountains.

At the summit, visitors find themselves at the top of the Continental Divide, where waters flow either to the Pacific or Atlantic oceans. Here, a well-marked viewing area and trailhead invite travelers to stop and soak in the panoramic views, explore the surrounding alpine environment, or simply enjoy a quiet moment in one of Colorado's most majestic settings. Interpretive signs provide insights into the area's geological and historical significance, including its role during Colorado's silver mining boom and the origin of its name, commemorating the Fourth of July.

Independence Pass is not only a journey through stunning landscapes but also a gateway to outdoor recreation. Hiking trails dot the area, leading adventurers to secluded alpine lakes, wildflower-filled meadows, and rugged peaks. Climbers and mountaineers are drawn to the challenging routes along the pass, while cyclists often tackle the road's steep grades for the ultimate test of endurance and skill.

The area's rich history is palpable, with remnants of old mining operations and the ghost town of Independence, where visitors can wander through the remains of a once-thriving community, offering a glimpse into Colorado's vibrant past.

12. Dominguez-Escalante National Conservation Area

The Dominguez-Escalante National Conservation Area (D-E NCA), sprawling over 210,000 acres in western Colorado, is a stunning mosaic of red rock canyons, arid desert landscapes, and lush riparian areas. Named after the two Spanish explorers, Francisco Atanasio Domínguez and Silvestre Vélez de Escalante, who passed through the area in 1776, this conservation area is a testament to the region's rich history, diverse ecosystems, and striking geological features. It encompasses the Dominguez Canyon Wilderness and is managed by the Bureau of Land Management (BLM) with the primary goal of conserving its natural and cultural resources while providing opportunities for public enjoyment and education.

The heart of the D-E NCA is its extensive network of canyons, most notably the Dominguez and Escalante Canyons, which offer visitors a spectacular array of red sandstone cliffs, ancient petroglyphs, and diverse wildlife. These canyons are carved by the Gunnison River and its tributaries, creating an environment that supports a rich biodiversity. The area's vegetation ranges from sagebrush and juniper on the dry, upland plateaus to cottonwood and willow along the waterways, providing habitat for an array of wildlife including mule deer, bighorn sheep, and over 115 species of birds.

One of the conservation area's most compelling features is its array of historical and cultural sites. Ancient petroglyphs etched into the canyon walls tell the stories of the area's early inhabitants, while abandoned homesteads and mining relics speak to more recent endeavors to settle and utilize the land. These sites offer a window into the past and an opportunity for reflection on the human connection to these landscapes.

Recreational opportunities within the D-E NCA are abundant. Hiking trails wind through the canyons, leading adventurers to hidden waterfalls, secluded pools, and breathtaking overlooks. The area is also popular for camping, horseback riding, wildlife viewing, and, in certain sections, river rafting and fishing. The conservation area's varied terrain and vast open spaces provide a perfect backdrop for outdoor enthusiasts seeking solitude and a deep connection with nature.

13. Montrose

Montrose, nestled in the scenic Uncompahgre Valley in western Colorado, serves as a gateway to some of the state's most spectacular natural wonders and outdoor adventures. This vibrant community, with its rich history, diverse cultural attractions, and welcoming atmosphere, offers a unique blend of small-town charm and easy access to the great outdoors. Montrose's strategic location near the Black Canyon of the Gunnison National Park, the San Juan Mountains, and the expansive public lands of the Uncompahgre Plateau makes it a haven for nature enthusiasts, history buffs, and anyone looking to explore the beauty of Colorado's Western Slope.

One of Montrose's most renowned attractions is the Black Canyon of the Gunnison National Park, located just a short drive from the city. The park is famous for its dramatic, steep-walled canyon carved by the Gunnison River, offering breathtaking views, challenging hikes, and excellent rock climbing opportunities. The canyon's unique geology and the sheer depth of its gorge create a mesmerizing landscape that draws visitors from around the world.

Montrose is rich in history and culture. The Ute Indian Museum, one of the area's cultural highlights, offers insights into the heritage of the Ute people, Colorado's oldest residents. The museum's exhibits and programs provide a deep understanding of the Ute culture and its significance to the region's history. Meanwhile, the Montrose County Historical Museum chronicles the broader history of the area, from its early days as a mining and agricultural center to its development into the thriving community it is today.

Montrose also serves as a hub for outdoor activities beyond exploring the Black Canyon. The surrounding landscapes are a playground for hiking, mountain biking, fishing, and golfing in the summer, with skiing and snowshoeing taking over in the winter months. The nearby Gunnison Gorge offers world-class trout fishing and whitewater rafting, while the Uncompahgre Plateau is crisscrossed with trails suitable for off-roading, mountain biking, and horseback riding.

The city itself boasts a lively downtown area, featuring local shops, art galleries, restaurants, and breweries that showcase the creativity and entrepreneurial spirit of the community.

14. Black Canyon of the Gunnison National Park

Black Canyon of the Gunnison National Park, located in western Colorado, is a place of profound beauty and awe-inspiring grandeur. Carved through the fabric of the landscape by the relentless force of the Gunnison River, this deep, narrow, and shadowy gorge presents one of the most dramatic settings in the American national parks system. The canyon's sheer walls plunge precipitously down to the river below, creating a visual spectacle that is both imposing and mesmerizing. With some sections of the canyon receiving only minutes of sunlight a day, it's a place where shadows dance across rugged rock faces, and the forces of nature are on full display.

The park covers a relatively small area of more than 30,000 acres, but its unique topography and the stark contrast between the deep gorge and the surrounding landscapes make it a magnet for nature enthusiasts and adventure seekers alike. The Black Canyon is so named not only for the darkness within its depths but also for the color of the Precambrian rocks that form its ancient walls. These rocks, some of the oldest exposed formations on Earth, tell a story of the planet's deep past.

Visitors to the Black Canyon of the Gunnison National Park can explore the South Rim and the more remote North Rim, each offering distinct viewpoints and experiences. The South Rim features the more accessible visitor center and several overlooks, such as the dramatic Painted Wall viewpoint, which provides breathtaking vistas of the canyon's deepest chasms. The North Rim, less developed and more secluded, offers a quieter experience of the park's natural beauty.

Hiking trails within the park range from easy rim walks to challenging routes that descend into the canyon's depths. For the most adventurous, inner-canyon hiking and rock climbing offer an up-close experience with the canyon's formidable terrain, though permits are required for these activities to ensure safety and minimize environmental impact.

Beyond the visual spectacle and recreational opportunities, Black Canyon of the Gunnison serves as a critical habitat for a diverse array of plant and animal life, adapted to the extreme conditions of the canyon environment.

15. Blue Mesa Reservoir

Blue Mesa Reservoir, nestled within the expansive vistas of Western Colorado, is not only the state's largest body of water but also one of its most captivating natural attractions. Situated in Gunnison County and serving as a crown jewel of the Curecanti National Recreation Area, the reservoir's deep, cobalt waters stretch over 20 miles, flanked by picturesque landscapes that shift from sagebrush hills to dramatic cliffs. This magnificent reservoir, created by the damming of the Gunnison River, plays a pivotal role in water management for the region but has also become a premier destination for outdoor recreation and leisure.

Boasting over 96 miles of shoreline, Blue Mesa Reservoir offers an endless array of activities for water enthusiasts. It's a haven for boating, whether you're sailing, kayaking, or cruising on a pontoon. The reservoir's vast waters are also ideal for waterskiing, wakeboarding, and stand-up paddleboarding, providing ample space for everyone to enjoy their favorite water sports without feeling crowded. Fishing is particularly popular here, with the reservoir known for its abundant populations of trout and kokanee salmon, making it a favorite spot for anglers seeking their next big catch.

Beyond the water, the reservoir's surroundings beckon adventurers and nature lovers alike. Numerous hiking and biking trails wind through the Curecanti National Recreation Area, offering breathtaking views of the reservoir and the unique geological formations of the surrounding Gunnison Basin. These trails range from easy walks perfect for families to more challenging hikes that reward the intrepid with unparalleled vistas and serene wilderness experiences.

For those looking to extend their stay, Blue Mesa Reservoir is dotted with campgrounds that cater to both tents and RVs, allowing visitors to wake up to serene water views and enjoy starlit nights by the campfire. The area's clear skies and minimal light pollution also make it an excellent spot for stargazing, adding another layer of enchantment to the camping experience.

Blue Mesa Reservoir stands as a testament to the beauty and recreational bounty of Colorado's natural landscapes. It's a place where water's tranquility meets the ruggedness of the Western Slope, offering a retreat into nature that's both exhilarating and calming.

16. Ouray

Nestled in the heart of the San Juan Mountains of southwestern Colorado, Ouray is often hailed as the "Switzerland of America" due to its stunning alpine scenery and charming, European-style village. This picturesque town is surrounded by towering peaks and rugged canyons, offering a breathtaking backdrop that draws visitors year-round. Ouray's unique location, rich history, and plethora of outdoor activities make it a quintessential Colorado destination for adventurers, history enthusiasts, and those seeking solace in the beauty of the mountains.

Ouray is renowned for its natural hot springs, which have been a source of relaxation and healing for centuries. The town boasts several hot springs pools, including the Ouray Hot Springs Pool, which offers multiple soaking sections with different temperatures, set against a panoramic view of the mountains. These geothermal waters provide a serene escape, particularly after a day of hiking, ice climbing, or exploring the town's historic district.

The town's history is deeply entwined with the mining boom of the late 19th and early 20th centuries, and evidence of this era can be seen throughout Ouray. The Ouray County Museum, housed in the former St. Joseph's Miners' Hospital, offers a glimpse into the town's past, showcasing artifacts and exhibits on mining, ranching, and the daily life of early settlers. Additionally, the Bachelor-Syracuse Mine Tour provides an opportunity to venture into a real silver mine, offering insights into the hardrock mining process and the lives of miners.

Outdoor enthusiasts will find no shortage of activities in Ouray. Beyond ice climbing, the area offers exceptional hiking, with trails leading to waterfalls, high alpine meadows, and scenic overlooks. The Box Canyon Waterfall & Park, just a short walk from downtown, is a must-visit natural wonder, where water roars through a narrow quartzite canyon, showcasing the power and beauty of nature.

Ouray's blend of natural beauty, rich history, and outdoor adventure creates a captivating destination that embodies the spirit of the Rocky Mountains. Whether soaking in hot springs, climbing frozen waterfalls, or simply enjoying the alpine scenery, visitors to Ouray experience a slice of Colorado that is as enchanting as it is exhilarating.

17. Ouray Ice Park

The Ouray Ice Park is a world-renowned ice climbing destination, ingeniously carved into the Uncompahgre Gorge within walking distance from the historic town of Ouray, Colorado. Emerging from a community-driven initiative, the park utilizes the natural geography and winter conditions of the gorge to create an ice climber's dream, boasting over a mile of terrain equipped with more than 100 man-made ice and mixed climbs. This transformation of the gorge into an ice climbing mecca each winter is a testament to Ouray's innovative spirit and commitment to outdoor sports.

Unique in its accessibility and scale, the Ouray Ice Park offers a variety of routes that cater to climbers of all skill levels, from beginners taking their first swings to elite athletes refining their technique. The park operates through the concerted effort of volunteers and staff who manipulate the flow of water from overhead irrigation systems to ensure the consistent formation of ice across the gorge. This controlled process not only maintains the quality and safety of the climbing routes but also extends the ice climbing season well beyond what natural conditions would allow.

Admission to the Ouray Ice Park is free, underlining the community's dedication to sharing the joy and challenge of ice climbing with as many people as possible. The park's democratic ethos and the sheer beauty of its icy formations against the backdrop of the San Juan Mountains have helped it gain international acclaim, drawing climbers from around the globe.

The highlight of the season is the Ouray Ice Festival, an annual event that celebrates the sport of ice climbing with competitions, clinics, gear expos, and social gatherings. This festival not only showcases the best in ice climbing talent but also fosters a sense of community and camaraderie among participants and spectators alike. It serves as a vibrant reminder of the park's origins as a grassroots project and its ongoing role as a gathering place for the ice climbing community.

Beyond its significance as a sporting venue, the Ouray Ice Park contributes to the local economy by attracting visitors to the area during the winter months, a time when tourism might otherwise dwindle.

18. Million Dollar Highway

The Million Dollar Highway, part of the U.S. Route 550 corridor running through southwestern Colorado, is an engineering marvel that offers one of the most breathtaking drives in the United States. Stretching approximately 25 miles from Ouray to Silverton, this segment of road is enveloped within the San Juan Mountains, famed for its jaw-dropping vistas, precarious turns, and steep inclines. The origins of its name are steeped in folklore, with some attributing it to the cost of construction, while others suggest it refers to the amount of gold ore that remained in the roadway's fill. Regardless of its origins, the Million Dollar Highway provides a journey that is truly priceless.

The drive is renowned for its scenic beauty, traversing through areas rich in history, marked by the legacy of Colorado's mining era. It climbs up and over three mountain passes: Red Mountain Pass, Molas Pass, and Coal Bank Pass, each offering their own unique and spectacular panoramic views. As drivers ascend Red Mountain Pass, they encounter the highway's most notorious section, characterized by sharp curves and sheer drop-offs without guardrails, demanding full attention and careful navigation.

Beyond the adrenaline-inducing aspects of the drive, the Million Dollar Highway winds through landscapes that are a photographer's dream. From verdant valleys dotted with wildflowers to rugged mountain peaks capped with snow, the route showcases the diverse beauty of the Colorado Rockies. Autumn brings a particularly magical transformation, with the aspen trees turning brilliant shades of gold and orange, creating a striking contrast against the evergreen backdrop.

Historic towns like Ouray, also known as the "Switzerland of America," and Silverton, a preserved Victorian mining town, bookend the journey, offering travelers a glimpse into Colorado's rich mining history and the opportunity to explore local shops, museums, and restaurants. The route is also a gateway to outdoor adventures, including hiking, skiing, and hot springs, making it a year-round destination for those seeking both thrills and relaxation.

19. San Juan Skyway Scenic Byway

The San Juan Skyway Scenic Byway, often heralded as one of the most scenic drives in America, offers a 236-mile loop through the heart of Colorado's San Juan Mountains, encapsulating the essence of the Rocky Mountain wilderness with its awe-inspiring landscapes and rich cultural heritage. This magnificent route winds through towering mountain peaks, historic mining towns, verdant valleys, and alongside rushing rivers, offering an ever-changing panorama that captivates and enchants travelers.

Beginning in Durango, a town famous for the Durango & Silverton Narrow Gauge Railroad, the Skyway takes visitors north to Silverton, a National Historic Landmark that boasts impeccably preserved Victorian buildings and a rich mining history. From Silverton, the route ascends to the breathtaking heights of Red Mountain Pass, offering stunning vistas of rugged terrain and wildflower-filled meadows, before descending into the quaint town of Ouray, often referred to as the "Switzerland of America" due to its picturesque setting and alpine charm.

Continuing west, the byway traverses the Uncompahgre Plateau to Ridgway, a gateway to outdoor adventures and the filming location for several John Wayne Westerns. The road then turns south towards Telluride, a world-renowned ski resort and festival hub nestled in a box canyon, surrounded by towering peaks. Here, visitors can explore the town's historic district, ride the free gondola for spectacular mountain views, or embark on hiking trails that lead to breathtaking waterfalls and overlooks.

The loop completes by heading through the fertile orchards and vineyards of the Dolores River Valley, past the ancient Ancestral Puebloan ruins at Mesa Verde National Park, and back to Durango. Each segment of the Skyway offers unique natural and cultural attractions, from the stark beauty of the high desert to the lush landscapes of the San Juan National Forest.

The San Juan Skyway is more than just a scenic drive; it's an immersive journey into the heart of the American West. It invites travelers to step back in time in historic mining towns, engage with the area's rich Native American heritage, and challenge themselves with outdoor adventures in some of the country's most pristine wilderness areas.

20. Black Bear Pass

Black Bear Pass, nestled high in the San Juan Mountains of southwestern Colorado, is a notorious off-road trail that offers an adrenaline-pumping journey coupled with some of the most breathtaking views in the Rocky Mountains. Situated between the towns of Ouray and Telluride, this narrow, winding path begins at an elevation of over 11,000 feet on Highway 550, near the summit of Red Mountain Pass, and descends into Telluride through a series of sharp switchbacks and steep grades. The trail is famed not only for its stunning alpine scenery but also for its technical difficulty and the challenge it presents to even the most experienced off-road enthusiasts.

The pass gets its name from Black Bear Road, which, according to local lore, was so named because it was "so narrow that a black bear would be scared to walk on it." Indeed, the trail is a test of nerve and skill, featuring tight switchbacks, loose rock, and sheer drops that can intimidate even seasoned drivers. Despite its challenges, or perhaps because of them, Black Bear Pass is a coveted destination for 4x4 adventurers seeking to test their mettle against the rugged Colorado terrain.

The descent towards Telluride offers unparalleled views of Bridal Veil Falls, Colorado's tallest free-falling waterfall, and the idyllic box canyon in which the town of Telluride is nestled. The sight of the waterfall cascading down the mountainside, with Telluride's quaint streets and historic buildings below, is a reward that makes the journey through Black Bear Pass unforgettable.

Black Bear Pass is only open for a short window each year, typically from late July to early September, depending on snow conditions. This limited accessibility adds to the trail's allure, making a successful traverse a badge of honor among off-road enthusiasts. However, due to its difficulty, it is strongly recommended that only drivers with high-clearance, four-wheel-drive vehicles and significant off-roading experience attempt the trail. Additionally, traveling in groups and carrying proper safety equipment is advised to navigate this challenging and remote route safely.

21. Telluride

Telluride, nestled in a box canyon amid the majestic San Juan Mountains of southwestern Colorado, is a town that seamlessly blends its rich mining history with modern luxury and outdoor adventure. Renowned for its world-class ski resort, vibrant cultural scene, and breathtaking natural beauty, Telluride is a year-round destination that captivates visitors with its unique charm and diverse array of activities.

The town's history is palpable in its well-preserved Victorian architecture and the storied streets of its historic district, where the spirit of the late 19th-century mining boom still lingers. Once a bustling hub for silver mining, Telluride has transformed into a haven for skiers, outdoor enthusiasts, and cultural aficionados, while retaining its small-town feel and sense of community.

Winter in Telluride is synonymous with skiing and snowboarding, with the Telluride Ski Resort offering more than 2,000 acres of skiable terrain that caters to all levels, from beginner slopes to challenging backcountry areas. The resort is known for its significant vertical drops, lack of crowds, and stunning scenery, with slopes that seem to plunge directly into the heart of the town. Beyond the slopes, winter activities include snowshoeing, ice climbing, and attending the annual Telluride Film Festival, which attracts cinema lovers from around the world.

Summer unveils a different side of Telluride, with its lush valleys and wildflower-strewn mountainsides becoming a playground for hiking, mountain biking, fly fishing, and festival-going. The town hosts a myriad of events, including the Telluride Bluegrass Festival and the Telluride Jazz Festival, drawing musicians and fans from across the globe. The gondola, a free mode of transportation between Telluride and Mountain Village, offers breathtaking panoramic views and is a favorite attraction in itself.

One of Telluride's most iconic natural features is Bridal Veil Falls, Colorado's tallest free-falling waterfall, located at the end of the box canyon. The hike to the falls and the surrounding trails offer outdoor enthusiasts a chance to immerse themselves in the area's stunning natural beauty.

22. Telluride Ski Resort

Telluride Ski Resort, nestled in the heart of the San Juan Mountains in southwestern Colorado, is celebrated as one of the premier ski destinations in North America. With its breathtaking scenery, expansive skiable terrain, and lack of crowds, it offers a skiing and snowboarding experience that is both exhilarating and serene. Spanning more than 2,000 acres and featuring over 300 inches of annual snowfall, the resort caters to enthusiasts of all levels, from beginner to expert, making it a perfect destination for families, solo travelers, and adventure seekers alike.

One of the distinguishing features of Telluride Ski Resort is its varied terrain, which includes long groomed runs, challenging steeps, and vast powder-filled bowls. The resort boasts more than 148 trails, serviced by 19 lifts, ensuring that skiers and snowboarders have ample opportunity to explore and enjoy the mountain with minimal wait times. For those seeking an adrenaline rush, the resort offers several terrain parks and the infamous Black Iron Bowl, providing advanced riders with the thrill of backcountry skiing within the safety of the resort boundaries.

The elevation at Telluride ranges from 8,725 feet at the base to 13,150 feet at the highest peak, offering one of the most significant vertical drops in North America. This elevation not only provides stunning panoramic views of the surrounding peaks but also contributes to the quality of the snow, which is famously light and powdery.

Accessibility is a key highlight of Telluride Ski Resort. The unique, free Gondola Connects the town of Telluride with the Mountain Village, allowing visitors to move easily between the slopes and the numerous dining, shopping, and lodging options available. This seamless integration of the resort with the local community enhances the overall visitor experience, blending the thrill of mountain sports with the charm of a historic mining town.

Telluride Ski Resort also stands out for its commitment to sustainability and environmental stewardship. Efforts to reduce carbon footprint, conserve water, and protect the pristine mountain environment are integral to the resort's operations, ensuring that the beauty of the San Juan Mountains can be enjoyed by future generations.

23. Lizard Head Wilderness

The Lizard Head Wilderness, a pristine and rugged expanse within the San Juan National Forest in southwestern Colorado, epitomizes the untouched beauty and grandeur of the Rocky Mountains. Encompassing over 41,000 acres, this wilderness area is named after its most iconic landmark, Lizard Head Peak, a strikingly peculiar rock formation that towers at 13,113 feet and resembles a lizard's head protruding from the earth. The wilderness is a treasure trove of high alpine environments, dense forests, meandering streams, and a diversity of wildlife, offering a sanctuary for those seeking solitude and an intimate connection with nature.

Characterized by its challenging terrain and remote trails, the Lizard Head Wilderness is a haven for experienced hikers and mountaineers. The area boasts a network of trails that navigate through varying landscapes—from verdant meadows dotted with wildflowers to stark, alpine tundra above the treeline. One of the most notable trails is the Lizard Head Trail, which traverses the wilderness and provides breathtaking views of the San Miguel and Wilson ranges, including the imposing Mount Wilson, Wilson Peak, and El Diente Peak, all of which are part of Colorado's famed fourteeners.

The wilderness is not only a destination for hikers and climbers but also a haven for backcountry skiers, photographers, and wildlife enthusiasts. The dense forests of spruce and fir, interspersed with aspen groves, are home to an array of fauna, including elk, mule deer, black bears, and a variety of bird species. The untouched nature of the area allows for wildlife to roam freely, offering visitors a chance to witness the inhabitants of the Rocky Mountains in their natural habitat.

Conservation efforts play a crucial role in preserving the natural beauty and ecological integrity of the Lizard Head Wilderness. Designated as a wilderness area in 1980, it is protected under the Wilderness Act, which ensures that the land remains undeveloped and that human activities are limited to those that do not alter its wild character. This commitment to preservation guarantees that the wilderness will continue to be a place of beauty, challenge, and inspiration for future generations.

24. Silverton

Silverton, Colorado, nestled in the heart of the San Juan Mountains, stands as a living testament to the American West's rich mining heritage. This quaint, historic town, once bustling with miners in search of silver and gold, has transitioned into a beloved destination for those seeking adventure, history, and the untouched beauty of Colorado's rugged landscape. With its elevation of over 9,300 feet, Silverton offers breathtaking mountain views and an authentic glimpse into the life of a late 19th-century mining town, preserved in time.

One of Silverton's main attractions is the Durango & Silverton Narrow Gauge Railroad, a historic steam-powered train that has been in continuous operation since 1882. The journey from Durango to Silverton traverses some of the most dramatic and beautiful landscapes in the state, including the Animas River Gorge, offering passengers a unique perspective on the region's natural splendor and historical significance. This iconic railroad not only connects visitors to the past but also serves as a gateway to exploring the area's outdoor recreational activities.

Silverton's charm is further accentuated by its designation as a National Historic Landmark District. Strolling through its streets, visitors are transported back in time, with well-preserved Victorian-era buildings that now house museums, galleries, shops, and restaurants. The San Juan County Historical Society operates several of these sites, including the old county jail, now a museum that showcases the area's mining history, and the Mayflower Gold Mill, a national historic landmark where visitors can learn about the gold milling process.

Adventure seekers are drawn to Silverton for its vast array of outdoor activities. In the winter, the surrounding mountains become a paradise for backcountry skiing, snowboarding, and snowmobiling, offering some of the most challenging and pristine terrain in the Rockies. Summer months open up endless possibilities for hiking, mountain biking, and off-roading on the alpine trails, including the famed Alpine Loop Backcountry Byway, which connects Silverton to Ouray through a series of scenic and rugged mountain passes.

Silverton's enduring appeal lies in its unique combination of historical depth, natural beauty, and adventurous spirit.

25. Durango and Silverton Narrow Gauge Railroad

The Durango and Silverton Narrow Gauge Railroad (D&SNGRR) is a historic marvel of engineering and perseverance, offering a journey back in time through some of Colorado's most breathtaking landscapes. Established in 1882 to transport silver and gold ore from the San Juan Mountains, this narrow-gauge railway has become an iconic symbol of the American West and a cherished heritage attraction. Running between the historic towns of Durango and Silverton, the D&SNGRR traverses a path through the remote wilderness, steep canyons, and alongside the rushing waters of the Animas River, providing passengers with an unparalleled view of Colorado's rugged beauty.

The journey aboard the D&SNGRR is more than just a train ride; it's an immersive experience that captures the spirit of the late 19th and early 20th centuries. The meticulously restored steam locomotives and vintage coaches transport passengers not only across the breathtaking landscape of the San Juan National Forest but also through time. The chug of the engine and the whistle of the steam as the train snakes its way up the mountain pass evoke a sense of nostalgia and adventure that is hard to find in the modern world.

Covering a distance of 45 miles one way, the journey from Durango to Silverton takes approximately 3.5 hours, offering ample opportunity to marvel at the engineering feats achieved in the construction of the railway. The track clings to the mountainside, crossing bridges and trestles, and navigating through tight curves and narrow passages, showcasing the ingenuity and determination of those who built it.

For many, the highlight of the trip is the stunning scenery. The train passes through areas inaccessible by road, offering views of pristine wilderness, towering peaks, and deep gorges. Passengers can witness the dramatic changes in landscape, from the verdant valleys and meadows around Durango to the alpine scenery and wildflowers near Silverton, all from the comfort of their seats or the open-air gondolas.

The Durango and Silverton Narrow Gauge Railroad is not just a train ride; it's an essential Colorado experience that connects visitors with the state's rich mining history, pioneering spirit, and natural beauty.

26. Durango

Durango is a vibrant town that beautifully marries its Wild West heritage with modern-day adventure and culture. Surrounded by the majestic San Juan Mountains and the verdant Animas River running through its heart, Durango offers an irresistible blend of natural beauty, history, and outdoor recreation that draws visitors from around the globe.

Founded in the late 19th century during the Colorado mining boom, Durango quickly grew from a small mining camp into a bustling town. Its historical downtown area, with well-preserved Victorian architecture, now hosts an array of boutiques, art galleries, restaurants, and craft breweries, reflecting the town's evolution into a hub of culinary and artistic innovation. The Durango & Silverton Narrow Gauge Railroad, a remnant of the town's mining past, remains one of its most iconic attractions, offering scenic journeys through the rugged wilderness to the historic mining town of Silverton.

Durango's geographical location makes it a paradise for outdoor enthusiasts. The Animas River provides ample opportunities for whitewater rafting, kayaking, and fly fishing, while the surrounding San Juan National Forest is a haven for hikers, mountain bikers, and climbers. The nearby Purgatory Resort, just a short drive from downtown, offers world-class skiing and snowboarding in the winter and transforms into a destination for mountain biking and hiking in the summer months.

Cultural events and festivals punctuate Durango's calendar, celebrating everything from its rich history and heritage to music, film, and local cuisine. The annual Music in the Mountains festival showcases classical and world music set against the backdrop of the Colorado Rockies, while the Durango Independent Film Festival brings filmmakers and cinephiles together to celebrate independent cinema.

But perhaps what truly sets Durango apart is its community spirit and welcoming atmosphere. Residents take pride in their town's heritage and natural surroundings, fostering a culture of preservation and respect for the environment. This collective ethos ensures that Durango remains not just a destination but a vibrant, living community that invites exploration, adventure, and discovery.

27. Mesa Verde National Park

Mesa Verde National Park, located in southwestern Colorado, is a UNESCO World Heritage Site that offers a profound glimpse into the lives of the Ancestral Pueblo people who made this region their home for over 700 years, from AD 600 to 1300. Spanning over 52,000 acres, the park is not only a natural wonder, with its high plateaus, sheer-walled canyons, and sweeping vistas, but also a cultural treasure, housing some of the best-preserved archaeological sites in the United States.

The heart of Mesa Verde National Park is its remarkable cliff dwellings, ingeniously constructed under overhanging cliffs. These structures, built from the late 1190s to the late 1270s, represent the pinnacle of Ancestral Puebloan architecture and include more than 600 dwellings, of which Cliff Palace is the most iconic. Cliff Palace, with its 150 identifiable rooms and 23 kivas (ceremonial structures), is thought to have been a social, administrative, and religious center for the Ancestral Puebloans.

Exploring Mesa Verde offers a journey back in time, providing insights into the daily lives, ingenious agricultural practices, and spiritual beliefs of the Ancestral Pueblo people. The park's well-designed tours and interpretive programs, led by knowledgeable rangers, enhance this experience, offering detailed narratives of the site's history and significance. Visitors can also explore the mesa top sites independently, where they can see remnants of pit houses and pueblos that predate the cliff dwellings.

Mesa Verde is not just about ancient dwellings; it's a landscape teeming with life. The park's diverse ecosystems, ranging from arid desert to lushly forested plateaus, support a variety of wildlife, including mule deer, coyotes, and over 200 species of birds. Hiking trails of varying difficulty offer visitors the chance to immerse themselves in the natural beauty of the park, from panoramic overlooks to quiet, secluded canyons.

Mesa Verde National Park serves as a poignant reminder of the resilience, ingenuity, and spirit of the Ancestral Pueblo people. It stands as a testament to human creativity and the desire to harmonize with the natural environment.

Western Slope Map 1 – Destinations 1-4

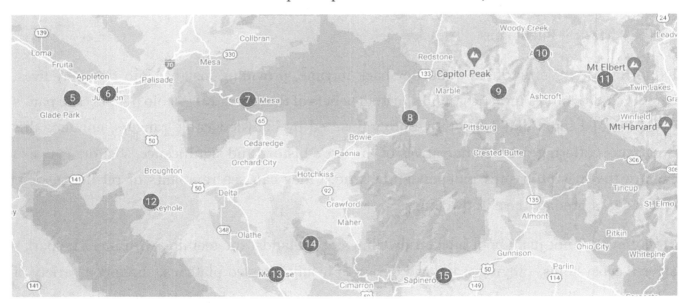

Western Slope Map 2 – Destinations 5-15

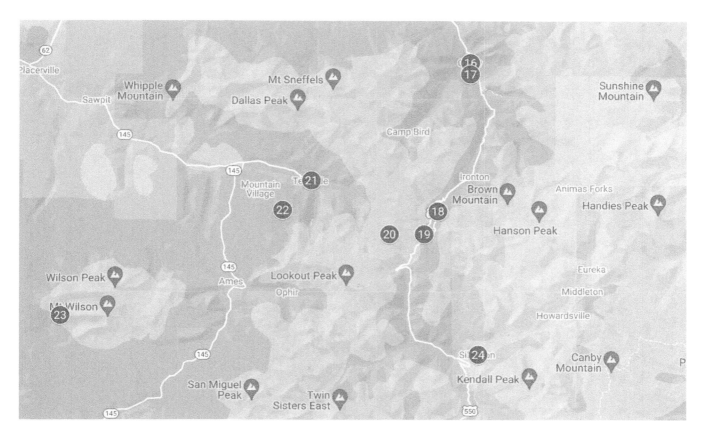

Western Slope Map 3 – Destinations 16-24

Western Slope Map 4 – Destinations 25-27

South

1. Buena Vista

Buena Vista, Colorado, nestled at the base of the Collegiate Peaks and along the banks of the Arkansas River, is a picturesque town that epitomizes the spirit of the Rocky Mountains. Its name, Spanish for "Good View," aptly describes the breathtaking scenery that surrounds this vibrant community. Buena Vista has become a magnet for outdoor enthusiasts, adventure seekers, and those looking to connect with the serene beauty of the Colorado high country.

The town's proximity to the Arkansas River makes it a premier destination for whitewater rafting and kayaking, offering some of the best rapids in the country. The river's waters range from gentle flows suitable for family outings to challenging Class IV and V rapids that test the skills of experienced rafters. Beyond the thrill of whitewater sports, the Arkansas River also provides ample opportunities for fishing, with its abundant populations of rainbow and brown trout.

The surrounding Collegiate Peaks, part of the Sawatch Range and named for Ivy League universities, offer endless opportunities for hiking, mountain biking, and rock climbing. Trails of varying difficulty lead adventurers through lush forests, alpine meadows, and up to the summits of some of Colorado's highest peaks. For those seeking a less strenuous outdoor experience, the area's hot springs provide a perfect setting for relaxation and rejuvenation amidst the natural beauty of the mountains.

Buena Vista's charming downtown area reflects the town's rich history and sense of community. Historic buildings house a variety of local shops, cafes, and galleries, offering visitors a taste of local culture and craftsmanship. Community events, from music festivals to farmers markets, add to the town's lively atmosphere, inviting visitors and residents alike to gather and share in the beauty of Buena Vista.

2. Mount Princeton Hot Springs Resort

Mount Princeton Hot Springs Resort, nestled at the base of the majestic Collegiate Peaks in Nathrop, Colorado, offers a unique blend of natural beauty, relaxation, and outdoor adventure. This idyllic retreat, situated in the heart of the Rocky Mountains, draws visitors from all corners of the globe seeking to bask in its therapeutic hot springs, explore the surrounding wilderness, and enjoy the resort's luxurious amenities.

The natural hot springs at Mount Princeton have been a source of rejuvenation and healing for centuries, known for their mineral-rich waters that emerge from the earth at temperatures ranging from 70 to 120 degrees Fahrenheit. The resort has harnessed these geothermal waters to create a variety of soaking experiences, including creekside hot springs where guests can relax in natural pools along the banks of Chalk Creek, and the more developed soaking pools that offer stunning views of the surrounding peaks.

Beyond the hot springs, Mount Princeton Hot Springs Resort offers a wide array of activities for guests of all ages. The resort's location provides easy access to some of Colorado's most scenic hiking trails, mountain biking paths, and fishing spots. In the winter months, the area transforms into a snowy wonderland, with opportunities for cross-country skiing, snowshoeing, and snowmobiling in the nearby San Isabel National Forest.

Accommodations at the resort range from cozy lodge rooms to luxurious cabins and cliffside rooms, catering to different preferences and group sizes. Each option is designed to provide comfort and tranquility, allowing guests to fully immerse themselves in the natural beauty of the area.

Dining at Mount Princeton Hot Springs Resort is an experience in itself, with options that emphasize fresh, local ingredients and offer a taste of Colorado's culinary landscape. The resort's restaurants and bars provide settings ranging from casual to fine dining, ensuring that every meal contributes to the overall experience of relaxation and indulgence.

3. Salida

Salida, Colorado, affectionately known as the "Heart of the Rockies," is a vibrant and welcoming town that has seamlessly blended its rich history with a dynamic present. Nestled along the Arkansas River and surrounded by the majestic peaks of the Sawatch Range, Salida boasts a landscape that inspires adventure, creativity, and a deep appreciation for the natural world. This charming town has become a haven for artists, outdoor enthusiasts, and anyone looking to immerse themselves in the beauty and spirit of Colorado's high country.

The historic downtown area of Salida is a testament to the town's mining and railroad past, with beautifully preserved buildings that now house galleries, boutiques, craft breweries, and cafes. The creative energy is palpable, with numerous art studios and venues contributing to a thriving arts scene. Salida's commitment to the arts is perhaps best exemplified by its designation as a Colorado Creative District, reflecting the community's dedication to fostering creativity and innovation.

Outdoor recreation is at the heart of Salida's allure, with the Arkansas River providing world-class opportunities for whitewater rafting, kayaking, and fly fishing. The river's banks also serve as a picturesque setting for festivals and concerts, further enhancing the town's lively atmosphere. Beyond the river, the surrounding mountains offer endless possibilities for hiking, mountain biking, and skiing, with trails that cater to all skill levels and showcase the stunning beauty of the Rockies.

Salida's warm, welcoming community is the final ingredient that makes the town truly special. Residents take pride in their town's heritage and natural surroundings, fostering a culture of sustainability and respect for the environment. This collective ethos ensures that Salida remains not just a destination but a vibrant, living community that invites exploration, adventure, and discovery.

With its stunning natural environment, rich cultural landscape, and adventurous spirit, Salida encapsulates the essence of Colorado's Rocky Mountains, offering a blend of relaxation, recreation, and inspiration that is hard to find elsewhere.

4. San Isabel National Forest

San Isabel National Forest, sprawling across the heart of Colorado, embodies the rugged beauty and diverse ecosystems of the Rocky Mountains. Encompassing over one million acres, this expansive forest is a mosaic of jagged peaks, alpine lakes, and vast wilderness areas that beckon outdoor enthusiasts from around the globe. The forest includes 19 of Colorado's famed fourteeners, mountains that rise more than 14,000 feet above sea level, offering some of the most challenging and rewarding hiking and climbing experiences in the United States.

San Isabel's landscape is remarkably varied, ranging from the arid, cactus-strewn canyons of its eastern reaches to the lush, coniferous forests and crystalline lakes of its higher elevations. This diversity of habitats supports a wide array of wildlife, including elk, deer, black bears, and mountain lions, as well as countless species of birds and smaller mammals, making it a prime destination for wildlife viewing and nature photography.

The forest is crisscrossed with trails that cater to all levels of outdoor adventure, from serene walks through wildflower-dotted meadows to rigorous treks in the backcountry. The Colorado Trail and the Continental Divide Trail, two of the nation's most iconic long-distance hiking paths, traverse San Isabel, offering backpackers the opportunity to immerse themselves in the natural beauty and solitude of the Rockies.

For those seeking a less strenuous connection with nature, San Isabel National Forest offers numerous camping sites, picnic areas, and scenic byways. The forest's lakes and streams are popular destinations for fishing, boating, and kayaking, providing a peaceful retreat amidst the towering mountains.

San Isabel National Forest is not just a haven for outdoor recreation; it's a sanctuary that showcases the majestic beauty of the Rocky Mountains. Its vast landscapes inspire awe and provide a space for reflection, renewal, and adventure. Whether scaling its highest peaks, exploring its serene forests, or simply soaking in the views, visitors to San Isabel National Forest are treated to an unforgettable experience that captures the wild heart of Colorado.

5. Royal Gorge Bridge and Park

Royal Gorge Bridge and Park, located near Cañon City, Colorado, is a marvel of human ingenuity set against the backdrop of one of the most stunning natural landscapes in the United States. Home to one of the highest suspension bridges in the world, the park offers breathtaking views of the Royal Gorge, a dramatic 1,250-foot deep canyon carved over millions of years by the Arkansas River.

Spanning the gorge, the Royal Gorge Bridge stands as a testament to architectural achievement, stretching 956 feet across and offering visitors a unique perspective of the canyon below. Constructed in 1929, the bridge originally served as a tourist attraction and has since become an iconic Colorado landmark, drawing visitors from all over the world. Walking across the bridge, guests can marvel at the engineering feat and take in panoramic views of the surrounding mountains and the river far below.

Beyond the bridge, Royal Gorge Bridge and Park offers a wide array of attractions designed to enhance the visitor experience. The park features adrenaline-pumping activities such as the Royal Rush Skycoaster, which swings riders out over the edge of the gorge, and the Cloudscraper Zip Line, North America's highest zip line, offering a thrilling ride across the canyon. For those seeking a more serene experience, the aerial gondolas provide a peaceful journey over the gorge, allowing guests to enjoy the natural beauty of the area from a different vantage point.

In addition to its thrilling attractions, the park is committed to providing educational opportunities. Visitors can learn about the geological history of the Royal Gorge, the local flora and fauna, and the history of the bridge itself through various exhibits and interpretive displays throughout the park.

Royal Gorge Bridge and Park is more than just an attraction; it's a destination that offers a blend of adventure, history, and natural beauty. Whether seeking thrills, wanting to learn, or simply looking to take in the breathtaking scenery, visitors to the park are sure to leave with lasting memories of one of Colorado's most remarkable natural wonders.

6.   Bishop Castle

Bishop Castle, an architectural oddity nestled in the San Isabel National Forest in central Colorado, stands as a testament to the eccentricity and determination of one man, Jim Bishop. What began as a one-man project in 1969 has evolved into a monumental stone and iron fortress that towers over the surrounding forest. This unique structure, built entirely by Bishop himself, has become an offbeat attraction, drawing visitors from far and wide to marvel at its towers, grand ballroom, and intricate ironwork.

The castle, which started as a family project to build a simple stone cottage, has grown organically over the decades into a sprawling complex complete with turrets, bridges, and a towering spire that reaches more than 160 feet into the Colorado sky. Bishop's use of native rock and salvaged materials, along with his self-taught construction techniques, have imbued the castle with a rugged, medieval appearance, making it seem as though it has emerged straight from a fairy tale.

Visitors to Bishop Castle are welcomed by the sight of soaring towers and the sound of clanging metal, as Bishop continues to expand and embellish his creation. The castle's interior is a labyrinth of stairways and rooms, each turn revealing a new surprise, from stained glass windows to a fire-breathing dragon made of metal. The highlight for many is the chance to climb to the top of the main tower, where panoramic views of the surrounding San Isabel National Forest stretch out in all directions.

Bishop Castle is not only a monument to one man's artistic vision and perseverance but also a symbol of the power of individual creativity and hard work. It serves as an inspiration to visitors, reminding them that with passion and persistence, even the most fantastical dreams can become reality. Free to the public, the castle invites adventurers, dreamers, and those curious about the limits of imagination to explore its towers and walkways, and to leave inspired by Jim Bishop's extraordinary vision and dedication.

7. Crestone Peak

Crestone Peak, rising majestically to an elevation of 14,294 feet, stands as one of the most challenging and revered mountains in Colorado's Sangre de Cristo Range. Known for its striking beauty, rugged terrain, and the sheer technical difficulty of its ascent, Crestone Peak is a sought-after summit for experienced mountaineers who are drawn to its mix of alpine climbing and breathtaking landscapes.

The peak is part of the Crestones, a group of high summits that also includes Crestone Needle, another formidable mountain. Together, these peaks dominate the skyline with their distinctive, jagged profiles, carved from conglomerate rock that gives them a unique appearance and climbing experience. Crestone Peak, in particular, is notable for its precipitous drops and sharp ridges, offering routes that require careful navigation and a high degree of technical skill.

Climbing Crestone Peak is no small feat. The most commonly attempted route, the South Colony Lakes approach, involves a long approach hike followed by steep, exposed scrambling and climbing in sections rated as Class 3 and 4. Climbers must be prepared for the mountain's loose rock, steep gullies, and the need for route-finding skills to navigate its complex terrain. The rewards for those who reach the summit, however, are immense: panoramic views of the surrounding Sangre de Cristo Wilderness, a profound sense of achievement, and a moment of solitude amidst the awe-inspiring beauty of the Colorado Rockies.

The area around Crestone Peak is also known for its spiritual significance. The town of Crestone, located at the base of the Sangre de Cristo Range, is a center for religious and spiritual retreats, home to a diverse array of monasteries, temples, and other spiritual communities. This unique cultural aspect adds another layer of allure to the mountain, making a visit to Crestone Peak and its surroundings a holistic experience that combines physical challenge, natural beauty, and spiritual enrichment.

For those drawn to the high places of the earth, Crestone Peak offers an unforgettable adventure that tests the limits of mountaineering prowess while immersing climbers in the profound beauty and tranquility of the natural world.

8. Rio Grande National Forest

Rio Grande National Forest, sprawling across over 1.8 million acres in southern Colorado, is a vast expanse of wilderness that captures the essence of the American West's rugged beauty. Named after the Rio Grande River, which begins its journey within the forest's boundaries, this national forest is a mosaic of high desert, lush forests, alpine tundra, and sparkling streams and lakes, offering a diverse range of ecosystems and landscapes for exploration and adventure.

The forest is a haven for outdoor enthusiasts, with its extensive network of trails that cater to hikers, mountain bikers, and horseback riders of all skill levels. The Continental Divide Trail, a highlight within the forest, provides some of the most scenic hiking in Colorado, traversing high mountain passes and offering breathtaking views of the surrounding peaks and valleys. In the winter, the forest transforms into a snowy playground, with opportunities for cross-country skiing, snowshoeing, and snowmobiling through its picturesque landscapes.

Anglers and water sports aficionados will find the Rio Grande and its tributaries to be prime spots for fishing, boasting healthy populations of trout. The forest's numerous lakes and streams also offer serene settings for kayaking and canoeing, allowing visitors to enjoy the tranquility of the water amidst the stunning backdrop of the San Juan and Sangre de Cristo Mountains.

Wildlife viewing is another cherished activity in Rio Grande National Forest, with its diverse habitats supporting a wide array of animal species. Elk, deer, bighorn sheep, and black bears roam the forest, along with smaller mammals and a variety of bird species, including the majestic bald eagle. The forest's commitment to conservation ensures that these creatures and their habitats are preserved for future generations to enjoy.

For those seeking solitude and a deep connection with nature, Rio Grande National Forest offers dispersed camping opportunities, allowing visitors to find their own private spot amid the forest's vast wilderness. Whether it's the thrill of outdoor adventure, the peace of nature, or the pursuit of wildlife viewing, Rio Grande National Forest provides an immersive experience into the wild heart of Colorado, embodying the state's natural diversity and beauty.

9.   Great Sand Dunes National Park and Preserve

Great Sand Dunes National Park and Preserve, located in the San Luis Valley of southern Colorado, is a natural spectacle that defies the typical mountainous landscape of the state. Home to the tallest sand dunes in North America, this unique park offers visitors a glimpse into a world where wind-shaped sand peaks rise up to 750 feet high against the backdrop of the rugged Sangre de Cristo Mountains. Spanning over 149,000 acres, the park encompasses not only the vast dune field but also alpine lakes, forests, wetlands, and grasslands, creating a diverse ecosystem where a surprising variety of plant and animal life thrives.

The dunes themselves are the star attraction, offering activities such as sandboarding and sledding, which have become popular ways for visitors to experience the landscape's unique beauty and fun. Hiking up to the top of the dunes provides not only a challenging workout but also panoramic views of the valley and surrounding peaks that are simply breathtaking, especially at sunrise or sunset when the light plays off the sand, creating a mesmerizing display of shadows and colors.

Beyond the dunes, the park's Medano Creek offers a rare beach experience in the middle of Colorado. In late spring and early summer, the creek swells with snowmelt, creating a temporary waterfront ideal for splashing, tubing, and picnicking. The surrounding areas of the park and preserve offer more traditional hiking trails through diverse landscapes, including the serene Medano Pass Primitive Road, which winds through aspen and pine forests, providing opportunities for wildlife viewing and connecting with the natural world.

Great Sand Dunes National Park and Preserve is not only a place of stunning visual beauty but also a testament to the power of natural forces. The dunes have been formed over thousands of years, shaped by the wind and water in an ongoing dance that continues to reshape the landscape. For visitors, the park offers a chance to explore and appreciate an extraordinary environment where the vastness of nature's creativity is on full display, making it a must-visit destination that captivates the imagination and spirit.

10. Alamosa

Alamosa, nestled in the heart of Colorado's San Luis Valley, is a vibrant small town that serves as a gateway to some of the state's most unique natural wonders and outdoor adventures. With the majestic Sangre de Cristo Mountains to the east and the San Juan Mountains to the west, Alamosa's landscape is a breathtaking canvas of contrasting colors and textures, offering endless exploration opportunities. This high-altitude desert valley, sitting over 7,500 feet above sea level, is home to a rich cultural history and a thriving community that warmly welcomes visitors from around the globe.

One of Alamosa's crown jewels is the Great Sand Dunes National Park and Preserve, located just a short drive from the town. This natural marvel, featuring the tallest dunes in North America, provides a surreal landscape for hiking, sandboarding, and simply marveling at the power of nature's artistry. The nearby San Luis Lakes offer a tranquil contrast with opportunities for bird watching, fishing, and camping under the stars.

Alamosa itself boasts a charming downtown area, where historic buildings house an eclectic mix of local shops, restaurants, and galleries. The town's cultural scene is vibrant, with events and festivals celebrating everything from local agriculture to Alamosa's rich heritage. The Rio Grande Scenic Railroad adds to the town's allure, offering scenic excursions through the beautiful landscapes surrounding Alamosa.

The town is also a hub for outdoor activities year-round. The Rio Grande River provides excellent opportunities for fishing and kayaking, while the surrounding national forest and wildlife refuges offer miles of trails for hiking, mountain biking, and winter sports. Alamosa's location in the San Luis Valley also makes it an ideal spot for stargazing, with clear, dark skies that reveal the Milky Way in stunning clarity.

Alamosa stands as a testament to Colorado's diverse beauty and adventurous spirit. Its blend of natural wonders, cultural richness, and friendly community spirit make it a destination that offers something for everyone, from the outdoor enthusiast to the history buff to those simply seeking a peaceful retreat in the beauty of the Rocky Mountains.

11. Lathrop State Park

Lathrop State Park, located just west of Walsenburg, Colorado, is a hidden gem in the state's park system, offering a unique blend of natural beauty, recreational activities, and serene landscapes. Spanning approximately 1,594 acres, it has the distinction of being Colorado's first state park, established in 1962. Nestled in the shadow of the majestic Spanish Peaks, Lathrop State Park provides visitors with spectacular views, diverse wildlife, and a tranquil escape from the hustle and bustle of daily life.

The park features two scenic lakes, Martin Lake and Horseshoe Lake, which serve as focal points for a variety of water-based activities. Martin Lake invites enthusiasts of all kinds, from boaters and water skiers to swimmers and anglers, with its warm waters being home to a rich population of bass, catfish, trout, and walleye. In contrast, Horseshoe Lake, designated as a wakeless water body, offers a peaceful haven for canoeists, kayakers, and those looking to fish in a more tranquil setting.

Beyond the lakes, Lathrop State Park boasts a wealth of outdoor activities. Its diverse landscape is a haven for hikers, bird watchers, and nature enthusiasts. The park's trails wind through juniper and piñon forests, across open meadows, and along the lakeshores, offering stunning views of the Spanish Peaks and the Sangre de Cristo Mountains. The park is also home to an abundant variety of wildlife, including deer, rabbits, coyotes, and an impressive array of bird species, making it a perfect spot for wildlife photography and bird watching.

For those looking to extend their stay, Lathrop State Park offers well-equipped campgrounds with modern amenities, ensuring a comfortable and enjoyable outdoor experience. Whether it's a day trip to enjoy the natural beauty and recreational opportunities or a longer camping adventure under the stars, Lathrop State Park provides a welcoming and diverse outdoor environment that appeals to visitors of all ages and interests.

12. Spanish Peaks

The Spanish Peaks, rising majestically in southern Colorado, are not only a striking landmark in the vast landscape of the American West but also a site of significant geological and cultural importance. These twin peaks, known as the West Peak and East Peak, stand as solitary sentinels on the eastern fringe of the Sangre de Cristo Mountains, visible for miles around and serving as a beacon to travelers and explorers throughout history.

Geologically, the Spanish Peaks are remnants of volcanic activity that occurred over 20 million years ago. These mountains are distinguished by their radial dikes, a unique geological feature where molten rock was forced into vertical fractures in the earth's crust, creating walls of rock that radiate outward from the peaks like spokes on a wheel. These dikes are not only fascinating from a scientific perspective but also contribute to the dramatic beauty of the landscape, drawing geologists, hikers, and photographers alike.

Culturally, the Spanish Peaks hold a special place in the lore and traditions of the indigenous people of the region, including the Ute, Apache, and Comanche tribes. The peaks were considered sacred, serving as landmarks for navigation and spiritual sites for ceremonies and rituals. The name "Spanish Peaks" itself is attributed to early Spanish explorers, although the mountains have been known by many names over the centuries, each reflecting the cultural heritage of those who have revered them.

Today, the Spanish Peaks are a destination for outdoor enthusiasts, offering a variety of recreational opportunities. The surrounding wilderness areas, designated as the Spanish Peaks Wilderness, provide a haven for hiking, camping, and wildlife viewing. The trails range from gentle walks to challenging hikes, leading adventurers through dense forests, alpine meadows, and to the summits, where breathtaking panoramic views await.

The Spanish Peaks stand as a testament to the natural forces that have shaped the Colorado landscape and a reminder of the rich cultural history of the region. They continue to inspire awe and admiration, attracting those who seek to explore their slopes and uncover the mysteries they hold.

13. Trinidad

Trinidad, Colorado, nestled at the base of the picturesque Raton Pass along the historic Santa Fe Trail, is a town rich in history, culture, and natural beauty. With its charming brick streets, Victorian architecture, and welcoming community, Trinidad offers a glimpse into Colorado's vibrant past while embracing the present. This southern Colorado gem, once a bustling coal mining town, has transformed into a destination for artists, historians, and outdoor enthusiasts, offering a unique blend of experiences that cater to a variety of interests.

The town's historic district, with beautifully preserved buildings from the late 19th and early 20th centuries, invites visitors to step back in time. The Trinidad History Museum, comprising several historic buildings including the famous Bloom Mansion and Baca House, provides insights into the lives of early settlers and the town's development. Meanwhile, contemporary culture thrives in Trinidad's burgeoning arts scene, with galleries, studios, and the Trinidad Space to Create initiative, which supports creative professionals and revitalizes the community through the arts.

Outdoor recreation in Trinidad is abundant, thanks to its prime location near the Sangre de Cristo Mountains and the vast, wild prairies of the Comanche National Grassland. Trinidad Lake State Park, a short drive from downtown, is a haven for fishing, boating, hiking, and wildlife viewing, with Trinidad Lake at its heart offering picturesque views and serene spots for relaxation. The park's network of trails also appeals to mountain bikers and hikers looking to explore the area's natural beauty.

Furthermore, Trinidad is emerging as a progressive town with a forward-thinking approach to community development and conservation, making it an attractive place to live, work, and visit. The town's commitment to preserving its rich history while fostering growth and innovation creates a dynamic atmosphere that honors its past while looking to the future.

With its historic charm, vibrant arts community, and stunning natural surroundings, Trinidad serves as a compelling reminder of Colorado's diverse appeal, offering something for everyone from history buffs and artists to nature lovers and adventure seekers.

South Map 1 – Destinations 1-13

Made in the USA
Middletown, DE
12 August 2024

58942413R00077